THE SUMMONS: ADVOCACY INSIGHTS FOR SYSTEMIC AND TRANSFORMATIVE CHANGE

Angela A. Allen-Bell
The Summons: Advocacy Insights for Systemic and Transformative Change

Published by Spines
ISBN: 979-8-89569-339-1

THE SUMMONS: ADVOCACY INSIGHTS FOR SYSTEMIC AND TRANSFORMATIVE CHANGE

ANGELA A. ALLEN-BELL

CONTENTS

Introduction   ix

Chapter 1   1
Prerequisites
Chapter 2   75
Advocacy Strategies

Conclusion   161
Acknowledgments   163
Post-Script   169
Notes   177

This book is dedicated to the 14-year-old Black girl who lost her life aboard The Recovery. That vessel held her captive after she was forcibly taken from Africa during chattel slavery. She is the alpha and omega of this book.

She is nameless, but she is not without an identity. She is a mighty symbol. Her stubborn feet sheltered the hopes of generations. Each blow to her ailing body collided with a defiant protest against degradation, inequality and indignity imposed by individuals and systems alike.

Her obstinate stillness is a smattering of what resistance can be. Resistance can be speech. It can be movement. Resistance can be subtle. It can be aggression. It can be long or short. It can be public or private. Resistance can be the simple act of maintaining joy and/or sanity. Resistance is defiance.

This anonymous Black girl did, in bondage, what most of us dare do as free people. She resisted. This book is both to honor her and to finish what she started.

INTRODUCTION

I am an expert on the interplay between race and justice who has developed a brand of lawyering that places restorative justice (RJ)[1] and transitional justice (TJ)[2] at the center of my work. My body of work includes injustices and abuses surrounding solitary confinement; excessive force; misconduct on the part of official actors; grand jury discrimination; Black juror suppression; prosecutorial misconduct; the criminalization of Black speech and dissent; excessive sentencing; wrongful convictions; black sites; various constitutional violations; and, racialized and political convictions. I have achieved tremendous victories and accomplished unprecedented successes, but little of what I have done in the twenty-six years that I have been a licensed attorney was ever taught in law school. This instructional void inspired this book.

The pleas from mothers, fathers, children, siblings and loved ones whose family members have been snatched away—much like that 14-year-old Black girl aboard *The Recovery*—are another impetus for this book. These individuals have been victimized by a player in the legal system or by one of its "processes" or procedures. Because of an injustice suffered by one they love, they find themselves working to achieve a just outcome in a system that often repels justice. This book attempts to prepare this population for what I term the "underground railroad to justice." Stated differently, this book is also written for those who have involuntarily become advocates in and against a system that harms.

This book is also for those who voluntarily assume the role of advocates for change.

This book is also written for those who, like me, are in service to the next generation. These readers embrace the transition plan revealed in my book *Diversity in the Jury Box and Beyond: A Formula for Transitioning Louisiana's Legal System* and are ready to be groomed to do the work that a successful transition requires.

Despite there being divergent reasons for starting this advocacy journey, this book seeks to arrive at a common destination. *The Summons: Advocacy Insights for Systemic and Transformative Change* "summons" readers–lawyers and non-lawyers alike–to duty as change agents. *The Summons* begins by explaining the competencies that change agents must display. After those prerequisites are introduced, specific advocacy and/or transition strategies and suggestions are provided. This book approaches advocacy, transition and/or civic engagement through lawful and constructive means.

In my book, *Under Indictment: Race, Juries & Justice in Louisiana*, I conducted an audit, inquest and assessment of Louisiana's legal system. My study determined Louisiana's post-emancipation legal system to be a system that allocates rewards and metes out punishments along racial lines. Tragically, systemic racism was not the only finding. *Under Indictment* also concludes that collective inequities and infirmities produced a legal system that has "speed as its heart, profits as its soul, caste as its pulse and callousness as its aorta."

"There is no chemistry in time to transmute wrong into right."[3] If change is desired, it will have to be commandeered by people. Either we embrace inaction or we accept the summons and begin the work of transforming systems that harm. A number of compelling reasons favor acceptance of this summons, the first of which is the dictates of the Declaration of Independence:

> [A]ll Men are created equal...they are endowed...with certain unalienable Rights, that...are Life, Liberty, and the Pursuit of Happiness–That to secure these Rights, Governments are instituted among Men, deriving their just Powers from the Consent of the Governed, that whenever any Form of Government becomes destructive of these Ends, it is the Right of the People to alter or to abolish it, and to institute new Government, laying its Foundation on such Principles, and organizing its Powers in such Form, as to them shall seem most likely to effect their Safety and Happiness....when a long Train of Abuses and Usurpations...evinces a Design to reduce them under absolute Despotism, it is their Right, it is their Duty, to throw off such Government, and to provide new Guards for their future Security.

The Declaration demands action in the face of destructive systems. An additional reason for accepting this summons is found in the Louisiana State Constitution. It recognizes people participation as a part of the governmental design:

> All government...originates with the people, is founded on their will alone, and is instituted to protect the rights of the individual and for the good of the whole. Its only legitimate ends are to secure justice for all, preserve peace, protect the rights, and promote the happiness and general welfare of the people.[4]

This is also the vision behind Louisiana's unique legal system. There are many civil law jurisdictions around the globe, but

Louisiana is the only state in the United States (U.S.) to operate under a civil law system of government. The other states use a common law system that allows judges to have far more power than they do in a civil law jurisdiction. While codes are used under the common law system, they are not the starting point for law like they are in a civil law jurisdiction. Common law jurisdictions operate largely on precedent (prior judicial decisions). Judges determine the precedent to be applied and are, therefore, quite powerful. In Louisiana, we intend for power to remain with the people and for them to express their will to members of the legislature who, as an extension of the people, enact the laws that go into our codes.[5] Legislation is sacred here.

Human rights law provides another basis for acceptance of the summons. In his 2022 message for the International Day for the Elimination of Racial Discrimination, UN Secretary-General António Guterres, said "We all have a responsibility to engage in solidarity with movements for equality and human rights everywhere."[6] He urged attention to those experiencing injustice and asked that their concerns and demands be placed at the center of efforts to dismantle discriminatory structures. And, finally, in 2022 the United Nations (U.N.) Committee on the Elimination of Racial Discrimination called upon jurisdictions to take concrete and effective measures to eliminate racial disparities at all stages of the criminal legal system and to begin the work of confronting systemic racism.[7]

Lawyers have a special reason for accepting the summons. The Model Rules of Professional Conduct calls them to duty both as citizens, as well as when they are acting as lawyers. The preamble to the Model Rules imposes a duty to "seek improvement of the law, access to the legal system, the administration of justice and the quality of service rendered by the legal profession." The rules tell lawyers that, as members of a learned profession, they should aid the legal profession by being mindful of deficiencies in the administration of justice and work towards reforming the law and furthering the public's understanding of and confidence in the rule of law and the justice system.

Active participation in the human struggle has also been a consistent call of the country's great change agents and thought leaders.[8] For members of the faith-based community, action is a moral imperative. The Bible is replete with reasons why, such as Isaiah 1:17, which instructs Christians to "[l]earn to do good, seek justice, correct oppression, bring justice to the fatherless, plead the widow's cause." Proverbs 16:8 teaches that "Better is a little with righteousness than great revenues with injustice." Christ lived a commitment to the marginalized, afflicted and impoverished. It's impossible to emulate Christ and ignore this many marginalized, afflicted and impoverished people:

An image from the Historic New Orleans Collection's 2024 Captive State *exhibit.* Captive State *uncovers the historical ties between slavery and mass incarceration in Louisiana.*

A further reason for accepting the summons is out of concern and love for the state and nation. Civic participation is as much a demonstration of patriotism as is military service, voting or public service. There is also a growing Truth, Racial Healing and Transformation (TRHT) movement that calls for transformational and sustainable change.

A final reason for accepting the summons is allegiance to the Black Radical Tradition, popularized by the late Cedric Robinson. Black Radical Tradition celebrates the myriad of ways Black people have struggled to be free and to experience equality. Through this expression, Robinson conveyed that the yearning to be free is a part of a Black person's spiritual and political origins. To him, it is the essence of our international legacy of resistance.

In short, indifference is a decision.

While Louisiana is the setting for this story, this story should not be dismissed as a local one. For decades, Louisiana has had the highest incarceration rate of any of the U.S. states, which itself has the highest incarceration rate in the world. Racial hierarchies continue to shape life in Louisiana. Louisiana's criminal legal system continues to need transformation, despite the eradication of non-unanimous juries. From that vantage point, there is something very universal about what might have initially appeared to be a local story. This journey begins on local soil, but this is so much more than a local story. The lessons contained herein are boundless and transferable. This is a template for local, national and global transition and it comes at an hour of great need.[9]

You are hereby summoned to duty!

CHAPTER 1
PREREQUISITES

Whatever is unjust carries in itself the seeds of defeat and decay. Justice is irrepressible. No matter how you may trample it, no matter with what fortifications you may surround the structure which you build up in opposition to that great principle, its voice is never silent. It clamors from day to day with a force that is irresistible, until at last its voice will be heard and the structure, whose foundations rest upon its violation, will crumble into ruin, a corroboration of the maximum that 'Nothing is settled until it is settled right.'[1]

Advocacy is not about getting one's name or image in the public domain, advancing self-interest or acting without a larger strategy. "Advocacy is a ministry of influence using persuasion, dialogue, and reason to affect change. Advocacy seeks to address structural and systemic [issues]....by changing policies, practices, and attitudes that perpetuate inequality and deny justice."[2] A successful advocate can achieve change through compromise or persuasion. Advocacy doesn't have to involve conflict or confrontation. Often, the most successful social change work is accomplished through relationship building. Advocacy can be the sole method of change or it can be used in conjunction with other methods (as demonstrated in chapter two). Before assuming the role of an advocate in an existing system that harms—such as Louisiana's legal system—or as a change agent engaged in the work of transitioning Louisiana's legal system or another system that harms, some competencies must exist. They follow.

Visioning

Advocacy, transition or social change should never begin with an outward action. Instead, the work must begin in the stillness of a thought. Visioning is the act of imagining what the new improved thing looks like or what success looks like. In *Freedom Dreams: The Black Radical Imagination*, Robin D.G. Kelley, a professor of American history at UCLA, speaks to the power of the mind and the significance of visioning. Kelley writes:

> Without new visions, we don't know what to build, only what to knock down. We not only end up confused, rudderless and cynical, but we forget that making a revolution is not a series of clever maneuvers and tactics, but a process that can and must transform us.[3]

In their article, *Reflecting on Race, Racism and Transitional Justice*, professors Matiangai Sirleaf and E. Tendayi Achiume register legitimate concerns about utilizing TJ to transition to a society that is an improvement over what was originally in existence, but one that still fails to achieve equality and equity for people of color because it fails to integrate their concerns into the transition equation. This book rejects that. It, instead, holds a vision for a transition rife with "emancipatory power."[4]

Transition is not instant. It is gradual. Genuine transition is slow and tedious work that requires generational commitments. Incremental steps must be taken towards the ends of a total transformation. There is no accelerated track. As each incremental step is taken, change agents must work with a vision *for that step* and change agents much have the visionary fortitude to imagine how the incremental steps will connect to form the whole over time. Strategies must be tailored so work is, at all times, tactical, intentional and vision driven.

My vision for a transitioned legal system is detailed in my book *Diversity in the Jury Box and Beyond: A Formula for Transforming Louisiana's Legal System.* It is not important that you share my vision. It's only important that you begin your efforts with a vision for the new thing you wish to see after the transition and with a smaller vision for how you will address parts of the whole.

<u>Redefining Victim</u>

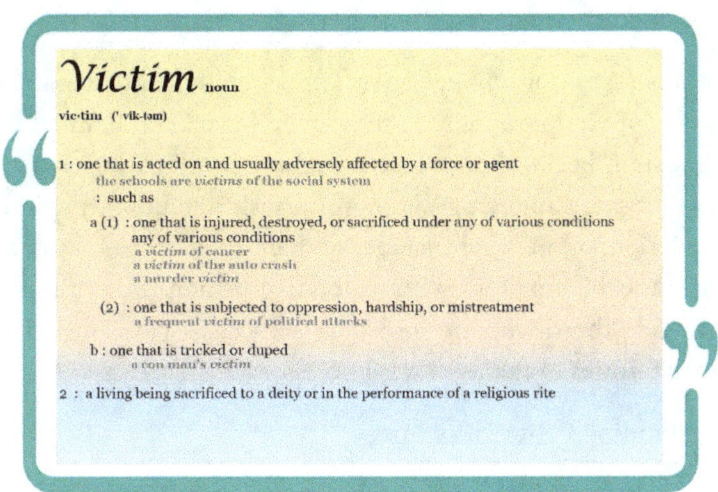

Since the late 1960s, there has been increasing public awareness of the ways crime harms crime victims. The Victims' Rights Movement has produced impressive results. In Louisiana, crime victims have advocates in some courthouses, a services bureau, a reparations board, support groups, access to restitution funds in some instances and more. According to The New Yorker's, *The Rise of the Victims' Rights Movement*, the Victims' Rights Movement, is "the child of an unlikely marriage of conservatism and feminism."

The consequence of this is a movement that has effectively elevated the voices and concerns of some and unintentionally ignored others. Because of racialized organizing, existing biases and stereotypes, Blacks are rarely viewed through the prism of "victim" even when they initiate civil litigation. In many instances, those who have interfaced with Louisiana's criminal legal system have experienced mistreatment. Many have been injured, destroyed or sacrificed. They are victims and no less victims than those directly impacted by crime. Yet, they are rarely viewed as such.

Upon this reasoning, change agents are encouraged to expand their definition of victim to include those who have been harmed by the carceral state because of prosecutorial misconduct; legislative failures; excessive sentencing; wrongful arrest, detention, prosecution or conviction; or, in other instances where they bear no fault in the circumstance. Consistent with restorative principles, victim should also include those who are forced to witness or vicariously experience the failures of the carceral state.

<u>Understanding White Supremacy</u>

White supremacy is the assumption that Anglo-Saxons are the first order of humanity. It assigns value, morality, goodness and humanity to the white group and deems them superior while casting people and communities of color as inferior, immoral, bad and inhuman. In their article *White Supremacy & Resistance*,

Darrell Miller and Carmen P. Thompson explain white supremacy with profound clarity. According to them:

> White supremacy is not just the Ku Klux Klan donning robes or burning crosses, but it can be. It is not just an individual act of racial discrimination, although it can be that, too. White supremacy is a collective set of codes, spoken and unspoken, explicit and implied, that society enforces through its institutions, governments, and legal structures in order to keep those deemed... [w]hite on top and other racial groups below them—with specific emphasis, in the United States, on keeping Black people at the bottom.

***

> White supremacy is subtle. It is historical, it is organic, and it is alive and well in the twenty-first century. In America, being [w]hite has long been the standard, the norm, the universal image and framework through which the nation's institutions have been conceptualized.

Understanding Race and Racial Discrimination

Change agents must understand why racial categories were created and they must be willing to reject the human hierarchy that Americans have been indoctrinated with.[5] The American Anthropological Association (AAA) defines "race" as a mode of classifying people and an ideology about human differences. In a 1988 statement, AAA stated that, "human populations are not unambiguous, clearly demarcated, biologically distinct groups." In other words, race is a man-made construct. The human hierarchy was designed to justify a system of benefits and consequences that is contingent on skin color.

Racial discrimination is "any distinction, exclusion, restriction or preference based on race, color, descent, or national or ethnic origin which has the purpose or effect of nullifying or impairing the recognition, enjoyment or exercise, on an equal footing, of human rights and fundamental freedoms in the political, economic, social, cultural or any other field of public life."[6] In order to fight racism, we must be proactively anti-racist.[7] We must also recognize separation however it presents itself amongst people and respond to it with inclusion. Connection is an important counter-response and a sure way of ending racism. Secondly, racial hierarchies must end. "The work of eliminating racism is a requirement if this experiment in self-governance and democracy is going to work."[8]

<u>Understanding Privilege</u>

Peggy McIntosh, a feminist educator, describes white privilege as:

> [A]n invisible package of unearned assets which [whites] can count on cashing in each day...an invisible weightless backpack of special provisions, maps, passports, codebooks, visas, clothes, tools and blank checks...[making] goals more accessible [and] harms more avoidable. While it does not ensure that every white person will win, it makes it harder for them to lose.[9]

Those impaired by white privilege start with the belief that whiteness is the norm and "whiteness is the site from which all things are measured and from which everything else deviates."[10] People other than white people can possess privilege too (though they often lack the institutional power to crush others with it in the way white privilege allows). Privilege does not confine itself to race. Heterosexual people can enjoy privileges that members of the LGBTQ community lack. Financially secure people can enjoy privileges that financially challenged people lack. Lighter-skinned Blacks can enjoy privileges that darker-skinned Blacks lack. Educated people can enjoy privileges that less educated people lack.

<u>Understanding Cultural Competency & Cultural Literacy</u>

Cultural competency is "the ability of individuals and systems to respond respectfully and effectively to people of all cultures, classes, races, ethnic backgrounds and religions in a manner that recognizes, affirms, and values the cultural differences and similarities and the worth of individuals, families, and communities and protects and preserves the dignity of each."[11] There has been a recent shift away from the "cultural competency" framework to instead talk about "cultural humility," which is considered the "ability to maintain an interpersonal stance that is other-oriented (or open to the other) in relation to aspects of cultural identity...."[12] The cultural humility framework suggests that work is ongoing. It chooses not to set a benchmark level of "competency" that can be reached.[13]

Those seeking to grow in these areas should become acquainted with Dialogue on Race Louisiana (DORLA) and/or America, My Oyster Association (AMOA). As Freedom Summer and the Civil Rights Act of 1964 captured the world's attention, Maxine Crump was making civil rights history locally. She enrolled at Louisiana State University in 1964 and was the first Black person to live on campus. That would not be her only claim to fame. She would later become the first Black, female disc jockey on Baton Rouge radio and the first Black, female news reporter on Baton Rouge television. Her most pioneering move would come later when she formed DORLA to eliminate racism through education, action and transformation.[14]

DORLA offers ongoing opportunities for formatted, facilitated and brave conversations around race. The original series includes six weekly sessions that explain the historical origins of racial hierarchies and the way they have been embedded into systems and structures to the detriment of citizens of color. This inclusive series offers participants a way to unpack the often false, and flawed narrative around race. Participants leave with expanded knowledge, language, understanding and clarity and are given tools for civil conversations around race and ideas for how they can be a part of change that is in line with the country's founding principles.

Maxine is unwavering in her belief that racism can be addressed in this country. She is emphatic that the hierarchy of human value that we know can be reconstructed if citizens agree to be participants in the process of transitioning to a new nation—one that no longer places "white citizens at the top of the social hierarchy entitled to a set of unearned privileges, leaving an unequal distribution of resources to citizens of color." Maxine also feels inaction or delay is detrimental to all people. She finds the results of a 2021 Gallup Poll showing that 64% of Americans believe that racism against Black citizens is widespread in the U.S. unsettling, especially when that 2016 poll indicated that fewer Americans felt that way (61%).

The increasing concern over racism and the continued disregard for a solution is destroying the health and stability of the country. Maxine calls citizens to prioritize a response. She suggests starting with a few questions, such as, "How was race constructed? How does race work presently? Who benefits from keeping racial hierarchies intact? What is the cost to the citizens and the country? What is the state of diversity in my environment? Who is in and who is out and why?" If you don't like the answers you get, Maxine says follow in her steps and blaze a new trail.

Many in the Baton Rouge community see Akosua Bea Gyimah as a modern-day Apostle who traverses the land speaking to Louisiana citizens about the importance of cultural humility to them, individually, and to the state and nation, collectively. Gyimah sees the pursuit of cultural humility as an act of good citizenship—a form of civic responsibility as important as voting and paying taxes. Her conviction led to the 2016 formation of AMOA, a non-profit she founded and of which she is President.[15]

AMOA's mission is to encourage individuals to understand the history of the country and the various struggles that punctuate the evolutionary journey of the country, as well as to celebrate the victories that have occurred along the way. AMOA challenges one to examine the understandings they hold because these understandings shape the way people interface with each other. In doing its work, great emphasis is placed upon diversity, equity, and inclusion (DEI).

AMOA fulfills its aims in a multitude of ways, such as hosting DEI trainings for citizens (including youth and seniors) and corporations; volunteering at cultural heritage celebrations; or, partnering with libraries and museums to promote their cultural programming. In 2021, AMOA, through a partnership with a library, launched "Building a Better America TODAY with AMOA," which invites the public (including students in secondary and higher education) to obtain a free online certification upon completion of training in the areas of DEI and empathy.

"Obtaining these skills allows individuals to become better versions of themselves. Simultaneously, a shift takes place in the state and nation when individuals truly begin to experience the America that we all deserve to live in—where life, liberty, and the pursuit of happiness for all, abound," says Gyimah. She feels businesses, organizations and governments must embrace this work as much as individuals. She says a necessary starting point is first acknowledging the need for cultural humility and forgoing the urge to disassociate with conversations centered around DEI. Instead, Gyimah encourages entities to "create opportunities for active listening so the people they serve can speak their truth about what it feels like as an inhabitant of certain spaces."

<u>Understanding Critical Race Theory</u>

Change agents must understand the meaning and purpose of Critical Race Theory (CRT). CRT was never intended for an elementary, grade school or young audience. The originators of CRT include law professors Derrick Bell, Kimberlé Crenshaw, Cheryl Harris, Richard Delgado, Patricia Williams, Gloria Ladson-Billings and Tara Yosso.[16] "Crenshaw—who coined the term 'CRT'—notes that CRT is not a noun, but a verb."[17] CRT recognizes that racism is not a bygone relic of the past. Instead, it acknowledges that the legacy of slavery, segregation and the imposition of second-class citizenship on Black Americans and other people of color continue to permeate the social fabric of this nation.[18]

Professor Crenshaw explains CRT as a critique of how the social construction of race and institutionalized racism perpetuate a racial caste system that relegates people of color to the bottom tiers.[19] CRT also recognizes that race intersects with other identities, including sexuality, gender identity and others.[20] Scholar Khiara Bridges outlines a few key tenets of CRT. It: [21]

- Recognizes that race is not biologically real but is socially constructed and socially significant.
- Acknowledges that racism is a normal feature of society and is embedded within systems and institutions...that replicate racial inequality.
- Rejects popular understandings about racism, such as arguments that confine racism to a few "bad apples."
- Recognizes the relevance of people's everyday lives to scholarship. This includes embracing the lived experiences of people of color, including those preserved through storytelling, and rejecting deficit-informed research that excludes the epistemologies of people of color.

Understanding the Messiah Complex

Those afflicted with a Messiah Complex have a need to redeem others. They view themselves as saviors. Their work has the appearance of service, but, in truth, it is about them. When you work toward transition or justice, work must be done alongside or in solidarity with marginalized communities, but never for them or as their savior. The latter is belittling, at the least, and racist, at most. Afflicted people hold a mistaken assumption that Black people are pacifists who have been accepting of their oppression and are in need of a speaker and leader. This is a false narrative.

"Harsh laws requiring cruel punishments for slave revolts would not have been needed if slaves were docile."[22] In actuality, "[w]hite communities lived in constant fear of slave uprisings."[23] Like the nameless 14-year-old girl to whom this book is dedicated, many of the enslaved resisted, imparting this spirit amongst their posterity. There were physical confrontations,[24] murders,[25] uprisings,[26] court challenges and various forms of work refusals including direct action or by suicide. Some followed the advice of abolitionists and voted for freedom with their feet (and simply escaped).[27] Some resisted with the written word, such as the Black abolitionist David Walker. In 1829, he penned *Walker's Appeal,* a groundbreaking treatise calling for the physical overthrow of slavery.

Right after slavery, in 1867, Blacks who worked discharging steamers organized a public protest after their demands for fair pay were ignored.[28] From the 1830s to the 1890s, Black men and women assembled through Colored Conventions where they strategized as to the attainment of equal rights. The Deacons for Defense and Justice (DFDJ), founded in 1964 in Jonesboro, Louisiana, protected the Black community from white vigilante attacks, as well as provided protection to white and Black civil rights workers. The DFDJ was comprised of Black veterans from World War II who believed in armed self-defense. About twenty chapters were created throughout Louisiana, Mississippi and Alabama.

As documented throughout this book, Blacks have made an uninterrupted pattern of demands for equity and justice in the various arenas of American life. There has been a multi-generational commitment to resisting oppression. Blacks do not need a savior; we need partners. Those who do this work must approach it with this understanding, remembering always the urging of Lilla Watson: "If you have come here to help me you are wasting your time, but if you have come because your liberation is bound up with mine, then let us work together."

<u>Distinguishing Between Opponents and Allies</u>

Advocacy work requires change agents to have the aptitude to identify allies who will aid them. It also requires the identification of opponents. They won't come with a warning label so change agents must have a keen ability to differentiate between the two. Using race as the sole matrix of who is an alley or opponent is a mistake that should be avoided.

The doubtful should first consider the plight of William Hayes, a white abolitionist, who, at great personal risk, helped many enslaved people escape slavery. Hayes was sued many times because of this. His work on the Underground Railroad depleted him financially, but he refused to cease his efforts.[29] Hayes was the face of a larger effort. When fugitive slave John Price was arrested in Oberlin, Ohio, white residents of Oberlin traveled to a nearby town, took Price back with them and hid him in the home of Oberlin College's President and later removed him to Canada.

A federal grand jury indicted thirty-seven of the people who freed Price. Two of them were tried: Simeon Bushnell, a white man, and Charles Langston, a Black man. Both were found guilty and sent to jail. More than ten thousand people, an overwhelming majority white, participated in an opposition rally. While these abolitionist efforts unfolded, some Blacks owned plantations and enslaved other Blacks during chattel slavery.[30]

Change agents should understand that, when the enslaved planned revolts, sometimes–such as in Lafayette, Louisiana–their efforts were undermined by one of the enslaved.[31] And they should know that some Blacks supported the Confederacy during the Civil War.[32] Change agents should also know that, when certain Southern whites resisted Reconstruction and used the legal system to re-enslave the newly freed Black population, some white men of goodwill did not respond with silence.[33]

Representative Morton was one of several who sought, *after* adoption of the Thirteenth Amendment, to expose and contest the misdeeds of the Confederates. Representative Morton said on the floor of the U. S. Congress:

> [T]hey returned the colored people to the condition of quasi slavery; they made them the slaves of society instead of being, as they were slaves of individuals. Under various forms of vagrancy laws, they deprived them of the rights of a freeman, and placed them under the power and control of their rebel masters who were filled with hatred and revenge.[34]

Representative Stevens followed suit:

> We adopted an amendment to the Constitution that slavery should not hereafter exist in this country except as a punishment for crime. Yet we find those States now reducing these men to slavery again as a punishment for crime, and declaring for every little petty offense the black man may commit that he shall be sold into bondage. So that even that constitutional provision which we made, and which was intended to knock the shackles off every man who was not guilty of a crime in the

United States, is avoided and got around by these cunning rebels.[35]

Representative Henry Wilson, another white man, observed:

> The poor freedmen, who a few months ago were leaping and laughing with the joy of new-found liberty...are now trembling with apprehension, everywhere subject to indignity, insult, outrage, and murder. During the past four months, in Alabama alone, fourteen hundred cases of assault upon freedmen have been brought before the Freedmen's Bureau. Thousands and tens of thousands of harmless black men, from the Potomac to the Rio Grande, have been wronged and outraged by violence, and hundreds upon hundreds have been murdered...The local authorities screen the murderers; the people protest against the punishment of white men for the murder of black men; and the murderers go unpunished.[36]

Representative John Kasson lamented about the "crimes and misdemeanors" perpetrated by the South: [37]

> [T]hey come here and claim...they must have their states' rights; that will let them; if they wish to whip them into exclusion from... voting...they are attempting, by that deception and trickery, odious and horrible in character, to defeat the wisest and most humane laws which we are passing for the protection of free citizens of the South. [38]

Some of these white Representatives choose to do more than just lament. An amendment to prevent the Confederates from using the Thirteenth Amendment's exceptions clause to continue practicing slavery and to further oppress Blacks was proposed. In support of this effort, Representative John Kasson had the clerk read this proposed amendment:

> [A]ny person or persons who shall hereafter sell, or offer for sale,
> or attempt to sell any person or persons whomsoever within the
> limits of the United States, or who shall make or issue any order
> for such sale, or who shall in anywise participate in such sale or
> attempted sale shall be held to be guilty of felony, and shall, upon
> conviction thereof, be imprisoned for a period of time not
> exceeding ten years or fined in a sum not exceeding $10,000, or
> both, in the discretion of the court....[39]

Representative Kasson exclaimed:

> I want this construction as a matter of justice to the Congress of
> the United States and the people who adopted the constitutional
> amendment, to show that they never intended chattel slavery to
> be reestablished under any circumstances....[40]

Jack K. Whitehead, Jr., the senior managing partner of the White-head Law Firm in Baton Rouge, is a living example to consider. Whitehead has served the legal profession with positions of trust since 1986 when he became an attorney. He served over twenty years in the Louisiana State Bar Association (LSBA) House of Delegates, a policy-making group of the LSBA; LSBA Board of Governors; LSBA Treasurer; LSBA Editorial Board for twelve years; and, the LSBA Labor Law Advisory Board. His public accolades are impressive.

Whitehead is a member of Super Lawyers and Stanford Who's Who recognized him as one of their notable professionals. Lawyers of Distinction recognized his firm's talent in labor law and Martindale-Hubbell recognized it as an AV Preeminent law firm. Garnering prestigious honors and the respect of the legal community is only a small dimension of attorney Whitehead. His public service and community work is a much more defining attribute.

Years ago, his frustration over the state of race relations in Louisiana compelled him to join the 100 Black Men of Metro Baton Rouge (100 BM), an organization grounded on four pillars–mentoring, education, economic empowerment and health and wellbeing. He is proud to be one of less than five white members. Much of 100 BM's mentoring efforts are directed toward Black males.[41] Whitehead is a staunch believer in the mission of the organization.

He lends his support in a number of ways.[42] When he learned that a 100 BM mentee was accepted to a local university, he worked tirelessly to find the young man a full four-year scholarship. On another occasion, he offered his Saints suite to bring mentees to a Saints pre-season game. He assists with summer job placement so mentees can learn life skills and he does whatever else he can to support the mission of 100 BM. Jack confesses that this act of service is a manifestation of his unique way of lawyering. "I believed a lawyer must earn the community's respect. Because of this, I have always been involved with civic, school, church and non-profits," he commented.

Change agents must know that when, less than five years after the Civil War, former Confederate General Samuel L. James approached the Louisiana legislature about contracts to lease convicts on his plantations, where he had not long prior held the enslaved, Black legislators were in office. They had a vote when he was awarded a twenty-one-year lease. "Of the twenty-five Negroes who were present and voting...all but one were in favor."[43] "Forty-seven white members supported the bill, while thirteen opposed it."[44]

It must be understood that, in 1913, white philanthropist and Pres-ident of Sears, Roebuck and Co. Julius Rosenwald instituted a program, conceived by Booker T. Washington, to construct rural schools for Blacks throughout the American South. He set up the

Julius Rosenwald Fund. "Black high school enrollment in the South increased from a few thousand students in 1920 to approximately 125,000 in 1931."[45] When the program ended in 1932, it had helped fund close to 5,000 schools in fifteen states.[46] "The Julius Rosenwald Fund supported the construction of 395 schools in Louisiana."[47]

Change agents should be aware of the fact that this dynamic can present itself on the bench. Donald Trump, a man accused by many of widening the country's racial divide, appointed Justice Neil Gorsuch to the SCOTUS. The source of the appointment combined with Gorsuch's ultraconservative reputation, produced anxiety amongst many. Justice Gorsuch, a white man, authored the *Ramos v. Louisiana* opinion that declared Louisiana's racist, non-unanimous jury system unconstitutional. In that opinion, he boldly concluded that the Sixth Amendment right to a jury trial—as incorporated against the States by way of the Fourteenth Amendment—requires a unanimous verdict to convict a defendant of a serious offense.[48]

In contrast, Justice Clarence Thomas, a man of Black complexion, wrote dissents in the cases of Louisiana's exoneree John Thompson and Mississippi's Curtis Flowers, two Black men. The late John Thompson was the source of adoration and inspiration to those like myself who work within Louisiana's Underground Railroad to free people from the grips of the carceral state. In 2017, the state got its way. John Thompson faced the capital sentence they manufactured for him years before he was exonerated from prison. The heart condition that he developed as an innocent man agonizing about his young sons and his looming death date snatched his life right when he was reclaiming it.

In 2008, John won a $14 million civil suit against the Orleans Parish District Attorney's Office. That came as a result of one of his prosecutors, Gerry Deegan, having a soul-cleansing conversation with his friend and former colleague, lawyer Michael Riehlmann, as Deegan reflected on his imminent death from colon cancer. During that conversation, Deegan confided in Riehlmann how he deliberately withheld blood evidence in a case he prosecuted many years earlier and that the evidence indicated that the defendant was not guilty. Thompson spent eighteen years in custody (fourteen on death row).

In filings before the SCOTUS, New Orleans prosecutors admitted they withheld evidence that John was entitled to when he was on trial. The evidence they withheld was the blood type of the perpetrator (which did not match John). The litigation established that, during the ten years prior to John's trial, prosecutors in the same office had withheld evidence that the defense was entitled to, resulting in four other convictions being reversed.

The late John Thompson & Angela A. Allen-Bell. Photo credit Briana Bell.

That judgment was reversed by the SCOTUS in a 2011 opinion written by Judge Clarence Thomas.[49] Thomas, writing for the majority, reasoned that this evidence did not establish that the district attorney was deliberately indifferent to the need to train the attorneys under his authority. The majority concluded that Thompson failed to prove a pattern of similar violations that would establish a policy of inaction sufficient enough to hold the municipality liable.

Like so many of the other justice-impacted victims of Louisiana's legal system, John accepted the summons. After that devasting blow, he got up swinging. He established Resurrection After Exoneration, a non-profit dedicated to providing reentry services, where he provided housing, transition services and mentorship to returning citizens. He received a prestigious Soros Fellowship to help launch a project to fight prosecutorial impunity in the legal system.

He used that forum to impactfully educate law students and legal stakeholders about the endless harms—to the accused, their families and society—that results from prosecutorial and/or other official abuses. John also lived the aims of this book. He believed in constructive civic engagement, he hungered for transition and he was skilled at advocacy. One of his many accomplishments was convincing the Innocence Project New Orleans to expand its mission to include advocacy on behalf of the wrongfully convicted.

Justice Thomas wrote the opinion in the Curtis Flowers case also. Flowers, a Black man, was tried six times by a white prosecutor who was discriminating against Blacks and preventing them from serving on his juries for no reason other than race. In his dissent, Justice Thomas wrote that it was a mistake to even give the court's attention to the case. He found the prosecutor's strikes race-neutral and defensible.[50] Justice Kavanaugh, a white man appointed by Donald Trump, authored the opinion finding that Mr. Flowers was a victim of jury discrimination.

These examples demonstrate why those who do the work of disrupting systems that harm must use a matrix other than race to identify allies and opponents. Allies should be identified by shared principles and mutual commitment to the aims of transition and/or justice. Oppo nents should be identified based on actions, inactions, expressions and sentiments that undermine the aims of transition and/or justice. No one group holds the patent on the struggle for justice and equality. In fact, as diversity enhances decisions during jury deliberations, diverse coalitions best serve the aims of transition and/or justice.

Understanding the Pace of Social Change & Making an Informed Decision About Your Level of Commitment

The late Angola 3 member Herman Wallace taught me one of the most valuable lessons of my lifetime. At the time he shared these insights with me, this revolutionary had survived life in a solitary confinement cell for about thirty-six years. He urged me to learn the difference between leaders and revolutionaries before I got too deep into the work of social change. Wallace taught me that a leader desires a change that can be accomplished in a season whereas the revolutionary measures victory in incremental terms and is prepared to wait for cumulative gains to ferment over time.

The late Herman Wallace & Angela A. Allen-Bell. Credit to the Justice-Impacted Photographer at Elayn Hunt Correctional Center.

In the interim, Wallace explained, the revolutionary does his or her best to redefine what is normal. The revolutionary continuously causes a shift in what the public once thought was the best that man could achieve and the revolutionary makes it uncomfortable for his contenders to function by breathing the stifling air of mediocrity. Transition and/or justice work is revolutionary work. I offer a few additional models to consider.

Pauli Murray was a lawyer, Episcopal priest, gender, civil and human rights advocate and author who associated with Langston Hughes and W.E.B. DuBois. As a student, she wrote a paper advancing a strategy for undoing the "separate, but equal" ruling made in the *Plessy v. Ferguson* (1896) SCOTUS decision. Her argument was used successfully in the *Brown v. Board of Education* (1954) case, but she was not given attribution.

She later became a colleague of Ruth Bader Ginsberg (RBG) who relied heavily on her writings in favor of using the Fourteenth Amendment's Equal Protection Clause as a means of achieving legal protections for women. RBG eventually claimed a seat on the SCOTUS. Pauli lived a life of relative obscurity much like Bayard Rustin who was a close advisor to the late Dr. Martin Luther King.

Bayard was a respected organizer, strategist and a strong force behind the civil rights movement. Bayard was the Deputy Director and overall logistical planner for the March on Washington for Jobs and Freedom in 1963 when Dr. King gave his famous, *I Have a Dream* speech. Bayard and Pauli were gay. Their sexuality made them liabilities to movements that they created and, as a result, they were written out of. What made them revolutionaries is what they did not do in the face of this. They did not quit. Without fame or recognition, they labored daily to disrupt norms and to introduce improved ones that had often never been imagined before.

Attorney Richard Sobol, a New York native and a Columbia Law School graduate, came to the South not long after passage of the 1964 and 1965 Civil Rights Acts for one reason—to advance the cause of civil rights vis-a-via the legal process. In the summer of 1965, he used his vacation time to work with the Lawyers Constitutional Defense Committee (LCDC), an organization formed by religious, civil liberties and civil rights organizations to send

Northern lawyers to the South to assist in the enforcement of newly enacted civil rights laws and to defend the thousands of civil rights activists who were arrested in connection with demonstrations, marches, voter registration efforts, protests or sit-ins.[51]

Attorney Sobol soon realized the needs of the people in Louisiana were long-term so his temporary stay became permanent.[52] At a fraction of what he could earn at his law firm, he devoted most of his life's work to the cause of justice in the South.[53] His birthright as a white man entitled him to privileges that he willingly surrendered. Sobol was a gasket on the engine of equality in Louisiana. When Gary Duncan's mother needed someone to mount a fight against Leander Perez, Sobol, not only accepted; he fought the case all the way to the SCOTUS. *Duncan v. Louisiana* changed a jury standard not just for Gary Duncan or the people of Louisiana, but the entire nation (discussed in detail in my book *Diversity in the Jury Box and Beyond: A Formula for Transforming Louisiana's Legal System & Other Systems that Harm*).

Sobol wasn't only a master in the criminal arena, he made effective use of the new Civil Rights Act of 1964 and Title VII, which prohibited racial discrimination in employment. Blacks in Bogalusa, Louisiana, recognized his abilities. That's why they called him to bring one of the first class-action suits involving Title VII. He sued the paper mill there and won on the premise that the use of tests in hiring and the use of seniority in promotions violated the Civil Rights Act.[54] He successfully sued on behalf of Black potato farmers in Lafayette[55] and Black sugar workers.[56] Sobol challenged jury discrimination and not in a symbolic fashion. He had to bear a heavy statistical burden to prove the underrepresentation of Blacks on juries in Louisiana federal courts.

He embraced the challenge as he fought on behalf of Black welfare recipients who were being criminalized.[57] Sobol fought against segregated schools[58] and against the deprivation of the vote.[59] He represented the first interracial couple married in Louisiana when they were being denied the right to marry.[60] He challenged housing discrimination.[61] He represented activists throughout the state and beyond who were arrested for making civil rights demands, charged with harassing offenses and denied constitutional safeguards.[62] Sobol demonstrated an indefatigable insistence on the full recognition of his client's civil liberties. Less than that was never suitable. A critical part of Sobol's success was understanding how to access and litigate in federal court.

He took time to speak at conferences where he trained other lawyers. After enactment of the Voting Rights Act of 1965, he transported Black voters to the polls. He sometimes participated in protests; other times, he was physically present as an observer so he could quickly secure the release of his clients when they were arrested.[63] In many instances, he could only collect fees after years of bearing the financial toll and labor of complex litigation. For the earlier part of his career in Louisiana, he worked with no full-time staff and only with the help of Northern volunteers who came at intervals.

Near the end of his life, Sobol compared his early career at a prestigious Washington, D.C. law firm where he and four lawyer colleagues worked for years on a single corporate dispute to his work as a civil rights lawyer in the South. "At the firm in Washington, I worked hard, but most of what I did never came to anything, certainly not to anything one could be proud of. In Louisiana, people who needed help would be depending on my work. Whether I did it and did it quickly and successfully meant the difference between jail or not...; integrated or segregated education; fair or discriminatory employment practices; the right to demonstrate or the denial of that right; access to public accommodations or the denial of access; the right to vote or tricks to nullify that right...."

Sobol admitted that the personal "impact of all this [work in the South]...was enormous." Yet, he declared it the more gratifying of the two worlds. Sobol was not celebrated, decorated or compensated comparably to the contribution he made. What drove him was the impact that one lawyer, familiar with federal litigation practice, could have on an entire nation. In 2020, he died at the age of eighty-two without the notoriety of even a Wikipedia page. Sobol is survived by his wife of forty-five years, Attorney Anne Buxton Sobol, who worked alongside him for many years. She urges change agents to see in this profile the possibilities of what they too can do if they are willing to be long distance runners like Richard.

Richard Sobol in 1991 at the release of his book, Bending the Law. *Photo credit Anne Sobol.*

The appetite of a revolutionary is quenched by evidence of a struggle. The recognition of time as a reservoir of rectitude sustains them. This isn't to suggest they don't deserve credit or recognition in their lifetime. They do. This only suggests that they are emotionally able to sustain their commitment in absence of it. Every movement has a colorful cast of characters. Revolutionaries are the shortest in supply. When you find them, you will know by the impact they make and the attention they never seek. In more abundant supply are opportunists, the ego driven or the profit motivated individual. Sprinkled amongst them are the sincere at heart and the leaders. Change agents must share the stage with this preordained cast.

<u>Understanding Credentials</u>

In February 1809, at the height of chattel slavery, a New York jury heard from witnesses in support of and in opposition to Amos Broad and his wife Demis Broad. The Broads were white and they were owners of an upholstery and millinery business. Those two privileges gave them the advantage in the criminal case that brought them to court. In a rare move, the Broads were defendants in a case involving mistreatment of enslaved persons. Several of the Broads' witnesses testified that they had never witnessed any ill-treatment of Betty and Sarah, enslaved property of the Broads, and they expressed that the Broads took good care of them. The state's witnesses testified that Mr. Broad kicked Sarah; whipped her with a horsewhip or rods; threw her in the snow; forced her to stand in cold weather for extended periods or until her feet were swollen or frosted; picked her up by the ear and drug her; and, forcefully rubbed Sarah's face into the carpet, causing her face to bleed.

The testimony revealed that some of this occurred when Sarah was only 3-years-old and that Mrs. Broad threw a knife at Sarah's head and engaged in other acts of violence towards her. Additional prosecution witnesses described Betty as an enslaved person who obeyed, performed her required duties and never tried to escape. Despite this, those witnesses recalled: that Mr. Broad stripped Betty naked and put her outside in the snow for an extended period (even throwing water on her at times); hearing Betty's agonizing cries as she was being beaten by Mr. Broad; seeing Betty locked up and starved for periods; seeing Betty's hands tied above her head for prolonged periods; observing Betty being forced to swallow laxatives when she was in good health; and, seeing Betty crying after beatings. They also testified to unspeakable horrors against the toddler Sarah. Jurors learned the violence was not corrective or warranted. Instead, it was done to degrade, harm and humiliate.

New York v. Amos Broad and *New York v. Demis Broad* resulted in rare assault and battery convictions of white owners for crimes against an enslaved Black women and her 3-year-old, Black daughter at a time when indiscriminate violence upon enslaved persons was both normal and expected. Mr. Broad, a white, slave-owner and father of five, was sentenced to jail time and a fine. Mrs. Broad was convicted of her crimes against Sarah and charged a fine. The point is not the outcome; it is what, or shall I say who, set this in motion.

Betty was, in the eyes of the law, a nothing. She was a thing; yet she had an impact. Betty's case led to accountability for her abusers, laid the groundwork for future legal protections for victims of violence and child abuse, forced a reckoning with the brutality of chattel slavery and provided support for eventual abolition. Betty did two things that are instructive. She found the only power she had and she leveraged it. That power was nothing more than the presence of mind to shout, cry or moan. The agony in those cries created witnesses and inspired vulnerable workers to file a complaint against their employers for abusing the enslaved and provided the courage needed by these hesitant witnesses to partici-pate in the trial. Beyond that, Betty, who had no education, training or social worth, undertook a second important step. She resisted inaction.

While advocacy work does require a skill set, it does not require formal education so no one should discount their ability to join the effort upon these grounds. Checo Yancy is amongst the ranks of Louisiana's most effective change agents. I have shared laughs with him inside the legislature, at hearings, in the governor's mansion and at countless community events. As you watch him engage in the work of change, the present muzzles any evidence of his former life as a justice-impacted resident of Angola for twenty years. When then-Governor Edwin Edwards signed the certificate of commutation of his life sentence in 1995, he claimed what freedom had to offer and did so with a vengeance.

As Policy Director of Voters Organized to Educate (VOTE), Yancy works alongside the Department of Corrections and the legislature, laying the groundwork for formerly incarcerated people like himself to strengthen their capacity to fight for their rights. In addition to continuing efforts surrounding reentry, Yancy has been front and center of many historic reforms in the state such as Louisiana's justice reinvestment initiative, securing voting rights for incarcerated citizens of Louisiana and ending non-unanimous juries.

Yancy urges those facing self-doubt to see, through his example, that anyone can be used by God to do his will on earth. Yancy furthers, "some of God's most effective workers have been people who lacked a formal pedigree." Yancy challenges change agents to believe in their ability to make an impact that ripples, but to also be self-aware so they are serving where best suited and not attempting to serve where are not best suited to serve. "The latter can be harmful," says Yancy.

In 1982, Kathe Hambrick was experiencing another reality. She obtained her Bachelor of Arts in English from California State University Long Beach and was enjoying corporate success. Circumstances prompted her return to Louisiana where her aging parents were. Not long after, she detected something harmful in the air, a form of pollution that had largely gone undetected. The state was spending millions in tourism dollars to promote a plantation industry that silenced, romanticized or misrepresented the stories of the enslaved.

This desecration of memory and interpretation instantly changed the trajectory of her life. It didn't matter that she had no formal training in this work. She secured a room in an existing plantation and started disrupting the false narrative. A fire at that site could not extinguish Hambrick's efforts. In 1994, Hambrick founded the River Road African American Museum (RRAAM), the first African American museum in Louisiana, as a means of telling those stories that weren't being (and largely still aren't) interpreted by the existing plantations.

She has since earned a Master of Arts in Museum Studies, founded the African Burial Grounds Coalition and is an author, independent museum consultant, curator, public historian, public speaker, and a leading cultural resource manager. Hambrick now has over thirty years' experience documenting Louisiana's rural history and culture. She readily admits that, when she decided to start RRAAM, she wasn't knowledgeable about museology. She is humbled at the thought that, over thirty years later, RRAAM has been sustained and is serving its mission well, particularly because of what she describes as disparities in the way state funding is allocated around interpretation.[64]

While formal education is not something you need in order to do the work of social change, Hambrick warns that other attributes are needed, such as dedication to a particular injustice, the ability to organize community members and proactive, visionary agendas that infuse notions of self-sufficiency. "People of color must end the cycle of dependency; we must stop depending on others to teach our children discipline, morality, good character, economics, and Black History, which, by the way, is American History and World History," says Hambrick.

A final example comes in the form of identical twin sisters who are small in stature, but colossal in impact. A summons calling a citizen to serve on a grand jury should not leave a person feeling as though they were part of an organized criminal syndicate, but that's what happened to the Howard sisters after one of them served. After reaching the conclusion that a Louisiana prosecutor had one of them cast a vote upon what she concluded was an incomplete set of facts, the grand juror felt deceived and violated. Worse, she felt forced into this conduct since she was required to participate under penalty of law. Although the grand jury does not render a verdict, but only an indictment—which is merely an accusation, or a decision that the person in question should stand trial to determine his/her innocence or guilt—this grand juror felt as if she had just laid the groundwork for the life sentence that was imminent.

Her conscience was unsettled by the thought of a grand jury only hearing one side of the case—the government's. After the process, she learned about the other side of the case through media reports and became sickened by what she was not told. Her identical twin soon sensed her affliction and began to bear her own version of it. Out of their helplessness came action. One twin sent nineteen heartfelt letters to officials directly involved in the case or the judiciary, such as judges (state and federal), the attorney general and members of his staff and the special prosecutor, pleading for someone to have the courage to do the honorable thing and end the prosecution. Each certified letter contained a return receipt. None of the recipients responded, prompting the second sister to mail over 500 more letters to people bearing responsibility for the legal system and the people of Louisiana, such as the governor, the legislature, congressmen, law professors, members of the bar, media and justice organizations.

She pleaded for them to "stand up for what is right" by demanding an immediate end to the prosecution. The pair estimates spending approximately $5000.00 of their personal funds on this campaign. They labor at the thought of trying to assign a cost to what this ordeal did to their health and emotional well-being. The accused party was ultimately released from custody, but the twins do not see this as a victory because the process outlived this particular prosecution. They live with the daily agony of more victims being produced. Now having researched the historical origins of the grand jury, they are convinced they and the accused would have been spared their anguish had the original intent of a grand jury been respected by state officials. They see that intent as the grand jury serving as a buffer, but only after gaining insights into both sides of a case. Records from the 1973 Constitutional Convention reveal support for this view.

Delegate Chris Roy described the grand jury process as "an arm strictly of the district attorney." Roy proposed that "at all stages of the grand jury proceeding...the accused shall have the right to assistance of counsel while testifying, a compulsory process for presenting witnesses...and the transcribed testimony of witnesses...." Other delegates agreed, saying they favored the accused having their side heard during grand jury proceedings. These supporters saw the process as being flawed because of the way the prosecutor, sheriff and judge controlled the selection of the foreperson and the evidence.

Delegate Woody Jenkins did not share Roy's views. Jenkins expressed comfort with a person having few protections during the grand jury stage. He reasoned, "your real protections are supposed to be in the courtroom." He continued, "Grand jury proceedings are not meant to be adversarial, but rather to provide the accused with the right to an independent determination of probable cause." The sisters feel they fall grossly short of this in a number of ways.

Louisiana's jurisprudence reveals a history of underrepresentation or exclusion of Blacks from grand juries. One Louisiana court observed, "[T]he uniform and long-continued exclusion of Negroes from grand juries shown by this record cannot be attributed to chance, to accident, or to the fact that no sufficiently qualified Negroes have ever been included in the lists submitted to the various local judges."[65] The court continued, "It seems clear to us that Negroes have been consistently barred from jury service because of their race."[66]

Louisiana's grand juries have also been sites of nepotism. A good example is Anne Butler's selection as forewoman of the grand jury that reindicted Angola 3 members Wallace and Woodfox in advance of their second trial. At the time, Butler lived in the prison community and was once married to Murray Henderson, the warden who led the investigation of the murder they stood accused of committing behind bars.[67] Butler reportedly wrote a book about the case and circulated it to fellow grand jurors.[68]

Worse, the "process" tilts in favor of one outcome because the "process" is driven by one side, which is the prosecution. With a newfound awareness of how long the grand jury has failed in its attempts at independence and fairness and how far from its original course it has deviated, the twins are admittedly dismayed by the inattentiveness to the matter given how high the stakes are when a grand jury is empaneled. Their lives are now devoted to the cause of grand jury transformation in Louisiana.

They are bothered by the toll visited upon a person who is indicted unjustly. That person is forced to mount a defense in order to fight a conviction. They think that should only happen when it's warranted, which means when grand jurors have all available evidence associated with the case or when they know they don't. The Howard sisters have a secondary motivation. They are aggrieved by the perception of grand jurors as automatons devoid of human emotions. They want that narrative changed. They want a system that favors greater disclosure for grand jurors and one that recognizes them as humans who can be traumatized by the weight of their adverse decisions when they are made in absence of all the facts or when they are made with the deception and prejudice that one side of a story can create.

For these collective reasons, these ladies, who lack any formal training for this work, have become effective crusaders for a Grand Juror Bill of Rights in Louisiana. The sisters plea for partners in legal system transformation in general or grand jury reforms in particular. They are confident that changes can be achieved if change agents are "creative, relentless, out-of-the box thinkers who don't underestimate their power."

Reverend Alexis Anderson is an ordained minister in the African Methodist Episcopal Church, a member of the East Baton Rouge Parish Prison Reform Coalition (EBRPPRC) and the founder and Executive Director of P.R.E.A.C.H., an organization that focuses on the three C's of literacy: competence in life skills, computerization and commerce. Anderson removes one hat and replaces it with another with the precision of a trained magician. If you walk into a courtroom in Baton Rouge, you are likely to find her there. If you walk into a council meeting, she'll probably be there too.

If a death has occurred in a Baton Rouge jail, you can probably find her at the side of the grieving family. When solutions to problems that stem from the intersection of mental health and poverty are being discussed, Anderson will likely be seated at that table. High visibility doesn't translate into a lack of focus in her case. She has over forty years of experience doing mental health advocacy work and there's no sign of fatigue. She monitors the Bridge Center for Hope and other mental health resources for those held in the East Baton Rouge Parish Prison with a vengeance.

Anderson offers sage advice to change agents concerning the core skills needed for advocacy work. Anderson says change agents should begin their work with a framework. Hers is ISAAC, which stands for Incarceration, Stigmatized, Asset, Attached Captives. "The heart of everything I do is empowerment so I focus on educational opportunities," explained Anderson. One way she empowers is by the way she recruits for court watch.

"Most organizations recruit individuals that will eventually be players in the system, such as law or criminal justice students, explains Anderson." Anderson continues, "Because of ISAAC, I believe those targeted by the system–people of color, LGBTQ persons, non-English speaking persons–should be recruited as court watchers." Anderson also stresses the importance of change agents identifying their approach to change. "I focus on prevention," Anderson tells. She continues, "I rather work on preventing the problem rather than work on fixing it after the fact."

Your methodology for advocacy should bear a connection to your specific strengths, talents and convictions. This will advance your advocacy efforts in indescribable ways. Successful advocacy work doesn't require an office, designated hours, a degree or title. It can be done in routine spaces or as a designated career. Being a successful change agent requires that one have a will to fight that is greater than the fear of consequences. It demands a concerted effort. It also requires that the change agent be: immensely knowledgeable of the matter at hand; have an achievable vision for change; disciplined; tactical and deliberate in actions undertaken (and never reckless or impulsive); persistent; motivated by collective improvement (not personal gain); and, compassionate and empathetic.

Understanding Geographic Disqualifiers

As he sat in his solitary confinement cell in a Birmingham, Alabama jail, Dr. Martin Luther King, Jr. responded to his many critics, many of whom were other Black ministers. In his *Letter from Birmingham Jail*, he challenged the notion that he was an outside agitator. Dr. King's rationale was two-fold. First, he explained that he was president of the Southern Christian Leadership Conference, a national organization with an affiliate in Birmingham, Alabama. In that capacity, he explained that he was invited into the state to participate in a direct-action program.

Secondarily, he explained that he was away from his home state and engaged in direct-action because that's where injustice was. Dr. King continued:

> Just as the prophets of the eighth century B.C. left their villages and carried their 'thus saith the Lord' far beyond the boundaries of their hometowns, and just as the Apostle Paul left his village of Tarsus and carried the gospel of Jesus Christ to the far corners of the Greco-Roman world, so am I compelled to carry the gospel of freedom beyond my own home town. Like Paul, I must constantly respond to the Macedonian call for aid. Moreover, I am cognizant of the interrelatedness of all communities and states. I cannot sit idly by in Atlanta and not be concerned about what happens in Birmingham. Injustice anywhere is a threat to justice everywhere. We are caught in an inescapable network of mutuality, tied in a single garment of destiny. Whatever affects one directly, affects all indirectly....Anyone who lives inside the United States can never be considered an outsider anywhere within its bounds....[69]

Long before King wrote these words, Northern abolitionists had been putting them into practice. The design of the Fugitive Slave Act of 1793 contemplated cooperation from Northerners who would have to catch or claim suspected fugitive slaves until the owner could claim his property. The property owner had to provide proof to the satisfaction of a judge or magistrate, either by oral testimony or affidavit that the claimed person was in fact one of the enslaved. The suspected fugitive had no rights and no ability to contest the allegation. Many Northern abolitionists felt jury trials could undermine fugitive slave laws. [70]

Consistent with this, a Pennsylvania Anti-Slavery Society Convention passed the following resolution in 1837:

> Resolved, That whatever difference of opinion may exist in respect to the degree and kind of obligation resting on the people of the free states, under the Federal Constitution, to return fugitive slaves to their masters, there is no obligation imposed on the

sovereign states, to surrender the liberties of any person without trial by jury.[71]

It was their belief that twelve Northerners, hearing from both parties, would not easily return people to a life of enslavement. Northern abolitionists may not have defeated the South when it came to trial rights for fugitive slaves, but they kept fighting to obtain protection through processes that would end the kidnapping of free Blacks or prevent the enslaved from being returned to enslavement.[72] Keeping these examples in mind, I encourage change agents to feel at home at any sight of injustice, whether it be a birthplace, familiar region or elsewhere.

<u>Understanding the Ripple Effect</u>

When officials from the U.S. Department of State had to communicate its 2022 update to the United Nations (U.N.), they spoke of a man seen through the prism of a wild mammal much of his life in Louisiana. Classmates and friends called him "Wolfman" supposedly because of his large teeth. Prosecutors used the fake alias in his indictment when, as a juvenile, he was tried for a 1963 murder in Louisiana.[73] When he was tried, the local media furthered the degradation with headlines like, "*Indict Negro in Slaying of Deputy Sheriff*" and "'*Wolf Man's' Arraignment Scheduled Here on Monday.*" The inhumanity changed forms after his conviction. "Wolfman" became inmate #71240. He remained that nameless, non-person for fifty-seven years. In 2021, he was finally granted parole and released from custody at seventy-five years old.

When the State Department spoke of him, they didn't call him "Wolfman." They told the U.N.:

> Regarding juvenile life without parole, the U.S. Supreme Court held in *Miller v. Alabama*...(2012), that a mandatory term of life without parole is unconstitutional when imposed on a juvenile

homicide offender. In *Montgomery v. Louisiana*...(2016), the Court held that the rule announced in *Miller* applies retroactively to defendants who were sentenced before *Miller* was decided....Most Federal prisoners who were serving life-without-parole sentences for murders committed while they were juveniles have been resentenced to terms of imprisonment that will allow them an opportunity for eventual release. In some cases, offenders have been released from prison.[74]

The State Department was referring to a man who did a singular act–challenge an injustice vis-a-via the *Montgomery v. Louisiana* litigation. Robert Kennedy had long ago forecasted this day for Henry Montgomery. He said, "Each time a man stands up for an ideal, or acts to improve the lot of others or strikes out against injustice, he sends forth a tiny ripple of hope and crossing each other from a million different centers of energy and daring, those ripples build a current that can sweep down the mightiest walls of oppression and resistance."

In their far-reaching communique, "Wolfman" suddenly assumed a name and human likeness. On a world stage, he was finally "Montgomery," the face of a ruling of constitutional proportions. Montgomery dropped a rock in a pond and got a current. Because of him, juvenile lifers in all fifty states have the opportunity for second chances. This power is ignited every time a change agent acts.

Henry Montgomery (right) being recognized by Bryan Stevenson (left) at the Legacy Museum in Montgomery, Alabama in March 2022. Photo credit Lloyd Jarrow.

<u>Understanding Systems</u>

The U.S. is a democracy. The federal government is divided into three branches to ensure a central government in which no one branch gets too much power. The same is true for the states. Amongst both, a legislative, executive and judicial branch exists. Within each branch are departments, such as the Department of Education or the Department of Justice. Within each department are agencies. For example, the Justice Department is made up of the Federal Bureau of Prisons and the Drug Enforcement Administration. Each of these systems have internal rules, policies and processes. Advocates must work with this level of specificity.

This is a point that Reverend Anderson emphasizes with great insistence. She explains, "in East Baton Rouge Parish, there are six courts that intersect: traffic, family, misdemeanor, city court and district court." Under this system, "a traffic citation can result in fees that can result in arrest that move a person though the various courts and, in doing so, open the floodgates of consequences, such as job and housing loss," she observes. "From there, she continues, "a person who was functioning independent of the system can become entangled in the system, simply because that individual contributes to revenue streams." "Change agents must understand how various aspects of their specific system work in tandem," she says.

For advocates working on issues related to justice-impacted communities, these resources offer guidance for navigating the "corrections" system:

- *A Guide to Helping Loved Ones in Georgia Prisons*, which guides families through talking to prison staff, requesting transfers and other issues that may arise while a person is in custody.[75]
- *Louisiana Informational Handbook for Friends and Families of People in Prison*, which explains the rules surrounding visits, communications, parole, clemency and internal operations.[76]
- The Prison Activist Resource Center indexes references to educational opportunities, reading materials, legal services, mental health treatment for the justice-impacted and the Jailhouse Lawyers Handbook.[77]
- Prison Policy Initiative's Advocacy Toolkit includes policy manuals for various institutions, a correctional contracts library and various housing authority policy exclusions for people with criminal histories.[78]

Understanding the Shortcomings of the Legal System

Many miscarriages of justice have a prolonged shelf-life because the public places unearned trust in the legal system. Change agents shouldn't doubt every judicial outcome, but they should approach them with caution more often than is done. Justice is not always correct or even concerned. Law can and does victimize people. Few people have been as bold as John Ashley in speaking this truth:

> [T]here is no crime known among men which it has not committed under the sanction of law. It has bound men and

> women in chains, and even the children of the slave-master, and sold them in the public shambles like a beast. Under the plea of Christianizing them, it has enslaved, beaten, maimed, and robbed millions...It so constituted its courts that the complaints and appeals of these people could not be heard...It has for many years drafted the Government and trampled upon the national Constitution, by kidnapping, imprisoning, mobbing, and murdering white citizens of the United States guilty of no offense except protesting against its terrible crimes....No nation could adopt a code of laws that would sanction such enormities and live. [79]

Because of the pace of justice in Louisiana and the unique way it merges with financial interests, race and class, change agents shouldn't, as a default position, deem a conviction, repeated denials of motions or appeals conclusive proof of guilt. If, after investigation, lapses surface, a challenge might be justified no matter what prior rulings say or conclude. Lead CBS News Correspondent David Begnaud and his team did exactly this and changed the trajectory of Vincent Simmons' life in early 2022.

Forty-five years prior, Vincent Simmons arrived at Angola on the word of teenaged, white twins who claimed they were victimized by a Black man in a rural Louisiana town. When the detective asked for a description of the suspect, one twin said "all n_ _ _ _ _s look alike." With that description, no physical evidence linking Simmons and no other witnesses or evidence, a mostly white jury found Simmons guilty and sentenced him to one hundred years for attempted aggravated rape. Simmons consistently maintained his innocence from the day of arrest throughout his incarceration.

Simmons personally obtained case records from behind bars, including documents that were hidden from defense attorneys at trial. Simmons, personally and through lawyers, filed repeated challenges (in both state and federal courts). Louisiana courts, indifferent to the unique intersection of race and rape in the South, upheld the conviction despite at least sixteen filings by Vincent that provided opportunities for courts to act in the interest of justice.[80]

CBS Reporter David Begnaud & Angela A. Allen-Bell in January 2022.

A fortuitous conversation between me and David Begnaud prompted a look into the case. He and his team were nearly blinded by the number of lawyers who had worked the case over the years, the volume of challenges made and the abundance of judicial rulings denying relief in light of the lack of evidence and obvious constitutional violations that Vincent had been the victim of. Thank God they viewed those rulings as commas and not periods. Their investigation of the case brought them to the official actors in the case. That changed the game.

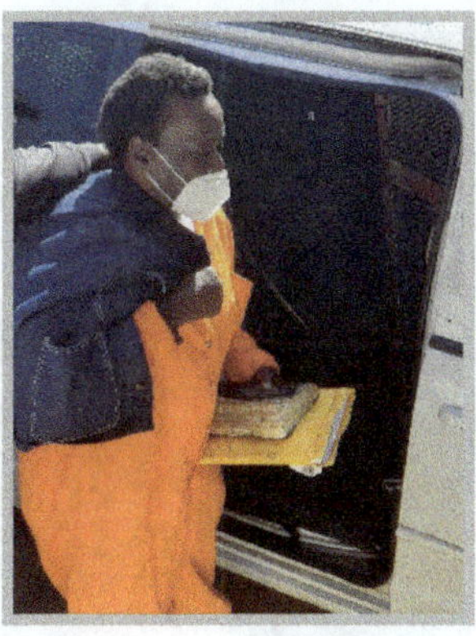

Vincent Simmons arriving to court in January 2022. Photo credit Angela A. Allen-Bell.

The world saw Simmons emerge from captivity on February 14, 2022, after Judge William "Bill" J. Bennet, in Marksville, Louisiana, did what his many predecessors failed to do. He cared about affording the accused party the process the constitution requires. He objectively considered the record then acknowledged that Simmons had been denied a fair trial in 1977 and he declared that a new trial was warranted (making no determination as to innocence or guilt).

Henry Montgomery, Tiffany Rainey, Attorneys Chelsea Hale, Angela A. Allen Bell, Reporter
David Begnaud and his partner Jeremy Tardo moments after Vincent was granted a new
trial. Photo taken by Matthew R. Foster.

Angela A. Allen-Bell exchanging a hug with Vincent moments after his release.

The history of non-unanimous jury challenges also bears proof of this point. In 1930, the SCOTUS was called upon to resolve the question of whether the Constitution allowed a jury of eleven to rule after one of the twelve seated jurors became incapacitated and the defendant agreed to a waiver. During its discussion, the court did not mince words in expressing its disapproval of a vote by a non-unanimous jury.[81] By the 1970's, the views of the court changed.

In the 1972 case *Johnson v. Louisiana*, the SCOTUS concluded that non-unanimous jury verdicts were permissible in some cases.[82] The Court thus held in *Johnson* that the Due Process and Equal Protection Clauses of the Fourteenth Amendment were not violated by Louisiana's non-unanimous jury law that allowed for a conviction based on a plurality vote of nine out of twelve jurors. In *Apodaca v. Oregon*, decided the same day as *Johnson*, the court likewise held that an Oregon rule that allowed for verdicts of ten to two did not violate the Sixth Amendment's guarantee of a trial by jury made mandatory on the states by incorporation through the Fourteenth Amendment.[83]

Apodaca is a plurality decision, which means that a majority agreement of the court never existed.[84] For nearly *fifty years*, these two "badly fractured" decisions became the basis upon which Louisiana appellate courts routinely declined constitutional challenges to Louisiana's non-unanimous jury system.[85] There was not even a word of *dicta* about the unsound ruling (and judges could have done at least this).[86] For the one hundred and twenty years that Louisiana used non-unanimous juries, Blacks were more likely to be found guilty by them than white defendants. Courts were aware of this, as well as the fact that the law was born of racist intentions.

They also ruled based on reckless conclusions about jury decision-making.[87] These opinions incorrectly suggested that a requirement of unanimity did not materially contribute to the exercise of a jury's common-sense judgment; that it perceived no constitutional difference between juries required to act unanimously and those permitted to return non-unanimous jury verdicts; and, they deemed it meritless that the viewpoints of minorities would be marginalized on non-unanimous juries. Finally, in 2020, the SCOTUS acknowledged that "*Apodaca* was [a] gravely mistaken" opinion justified by an "incomplete functionalist analysis of its own creation."[88]

Understanding The Risks

Being a change agent involves a lot more than joining a single march, making some social media posts or being photographed wearing messaged t-shirts. It is a life of grind, toil, obstacles, sacrifices, inconveniences and challenges that can bring personal risks. Many leaders or change agents have become targeted by those who oppose their efforts to achieve change. For leading a 1831 slave revolt, Nat Turner was hung, skinned and decapitated then grease was made from his flesh.[89] In the 1890s, Callie House, a formerly enslaved woman, formed the National Ex-Slave Mutual Relief,

Bounty and Pension Association, a national grass-roots organization that demanded the federal government pay pensions to the formerly enslaved. Her movement ended when federal officials falsely accused her of fraud. She was later indicted and incarcerated.[90] The list of artists, educators and activists who suffered under COINTELPRO–short for Counterintelligence Program–seems endless.

They include members of the Black Panther Party (BPP), Dr. Martin Luther King, Billie Holliday, anti-war activists and many others.[91] In 1923, Black nationalist leader Marcus Garvey was convicted on federal charges of mail fraud and later deported to Jamacia. In 2022, a jury acquitted New Orleans' new district attorney Jason Williams of charges he conspired to defraud the IRS with falsified tax returns and failed to file proper forms for large cash payments. During his campaign for office, Williams ran as a "progressive prosecutor." D.A. Williams said, the case "Was an effort to disparage me, and drag my reputation through the mud." He continued, "And now I personally felt the pain, fear, isolation, and disorientation of an abuse of power, the abuse of prosecutorial discretion. It was an incredibly sober experience to witness the power of an overbearing rogue prosecution."

Sobriety was short lived. On September 5, 2024, D.A. Williams was hauled into yet another unprecedented proceeding for a man of his stature. This time a legislative committee, in a state with a history of being deferential to prosecutorial discretion, questioned him extensively about his use of prosecutorial discretion when it came to granting post conviction relief in some cases. During this "process," this Black D.A. was even submitted to attacks and mischaracterizations by those who resent his open expressions about the need to "correct the sins of the past" or his identification as a progressive prosecutor who is unconvinced that overincarceration leads to public safety. Despite an excessively high rate of wrongful convictions and an alarming pattern of prosecutorial misconduct in the state, no other prosecutor has ever been subjected to this type of public degradation in the state's legislative chamber.

In fact, recent attempts to enact prosecutorial oversight legislation failed because Louisiana prosecutors collectively organized against it. As a collective, they apparently missed the notice of the hearing when D.A. Jason Williams, one of the few Blacks amongst their ranks and the only D.A. to openly acknowledge the systemic shortcomings of Louisiana's judicial system was hauled into the legislature by Republican legislators and the daughter of the former Orleans Parish D.A. whose office should have been subject of a hearing for his use of fake subpoenas on the unsuspecting public and the high rate of prosecutorial misconduct documented during his term. Social change requires a high tolerance for pain, a great level of endurance and the capacity to face rejection and persecution and to face much of this alone.

<u>Understanding Partnerships</u>

Collaboration sparks a synergy that can't be attained by an individual. Through collaborations, individual competencies are strengthened. Partnerships help with coalition building and coalition building is necessary if transformation and/or justice is to be achieved. A study of slavery era politics demonstrates how this works. Each pro-slavery state realized a collective effort was a better way of championing a cause. Once the Ordinance of Secession was drafted, Confederates used commissioners to visit sister slaveholding states for the purpose of strengthening the secession movement. The resulting coalition met at a convention in Montgomery, Alabama to form the Confederate States of America.[92] The coalition produced a tenacity that likely would have never been realized if the effort consisted of a few, individual, pro-slavery advocates.

Reverend Alexis Anderson elaborates further. "I welcome partnerships that aren't tied to common bonds, but common interests," says Anderson. She lives by the mantra: "no permanent friends; no permanent enemies; just permanent interests." This collaborative model brings the appropriate partners to the need and allows for multiple relationships to enter and exit as needed (i.e., sometimes an organization partners on a project but feels the next project isn't a fit for them organizationally)," Anderson explains. Anderson continues, "this approach allows us to build unlimited partnerships with limited permanent alignment." When considering partners, the decision should be tactical. There should be a mutual benefit and an identifiable gain from the partnership. Liabilities shouldn't be overlooked in the assessment. A few examples follow.

With the Faith-Based Community

The Angola 3 advocacy team sought to enlarge the conversation surrounding solitary confinement. On a national level, a partnership with The National Religious Campaign Against Torture (NRCAT) was formed. This converted a former criminal justice conversation into a biblical and human rights one and, in so doing, broadened the support base. Partnerships were also formed with members of the local faith-based community. One, the Rose Hill Church, pastored by Danny Donaldson, hosted a 2012 prayer service.

Attorney Nicholas Trenticosta speaks to the audience about the facts of the Angola 3 case. Photo credit Angela A. Allen-Bell.

The message Pastor Donaldson delivered that day reminded the Angola 3 advocacy team that the climb up a mountain with a huge bolder is exhausting and depleting and can only be finished with faith. He said getting to the top would seem like it required more physical strength than one possessed, but he encouraged us to increase our faith and push on until we made it. Pastor Donaldson said when we got to the top, God would reward our faith and we would be able to release the boulder and watch it roll, effortlessly. I remain steadfast in my belief that that message and the prayers that went up that night and many nights prior and after got us to the top of that mountain. Within a year of that message, boulders came crashing down that mountain. Herman Wallace emerged from forty-one years in solitary confinement. Four years later, Albert Woodfox emerged from forty-three years of the same.

Advocate Mada Clark-McDonald gives the call to action.
Pastor Donaldson observes before he delivers the message.
Photo credit Angela A. Allen-Bell.

Angola 3 member Herman Wallace's sister Justina Williams mesmerizes the audience with a gospel song. Photo by Angela A. Allen-Bell.

With Groups Having a Related Mission

Another partnership to consider is with groups whose mission speaks to the issue you are working on. An example is the Angola 3 coalition's collaboration with Amnesty International. That partnership led to a very thorough educational pamphlet, letter-writing campaigns, a petition drive, international awareness and an expanded base of support. The Unanimous Jury Campaign (UJC) was formed to get voters to cast a vote in support of a constitutional amendment that would end the use of non-unanimous juries in Louisiana. The UJC also utilized partnerships with many criminal justice stakeholders. These partners used their membership lists and resources to get voters educated and motivated to cast votes in favor of unanimous juries.

Amicus curiae filings ("friend of the court" briefs) are another benefit to result from strategic partnerships. They are filed with the court by parties who share an interest in legal issues. They can provide additional research or alternative positions to the court. More importantly, they let the court know that many others are concerned with and impacted by the issue at hand. They were effectively used through the various stages of the non-unanimous jury litigation. They were filed by such groups as The Juror Project, Center for Constitutional Rights (CCR), Innocence Project New Orleans (IPNO), Lawyers Committee Legal Defense

Fund (LDF), Voice of the Experienced (VOTE), and the Louisiana Center for Children's Rights (LCCR). Louisiana prosecutors employ this tactic a lot. It's not unusual to see the District Attorneys Association file an amicus brief *in support of* the prosecutor before the court on allegations of misconduct.

With Professional Organizations

Partnerships with professional associations are also encouraged. During the campaign to end non-unanimous juries, I received an email from then American Bar Association (ABA) president Judy Perry Martinez who observed the local work I was doing and expressed an interest in taking action at the ABA level. Along with the ACLU New Orleans director Marjorie Esman, Tulane University professor Heather Johnson and ABA officials, I co-authored the ABA's Criminal Justice Section Resolution and Report urging Louisiana and Oregon to require unanimous juries to determine guilt. The resolution passed at the association's spring 2018 Criminal Justice Council Meeting and changed policy at the association level. It urged Louisiana and Oregon to require unanimous juries in felony criminal cases.

Another example to consider is professional groups with a social justice mission, such as Architects/Designers/Planners for Social Responsibility. They launched a campaign asking their mainstream professional organization, the American Institute of Architects (AIA), to amend its Code of Ethics to ban the design of spaces intended for execution and prolonged solitary confinement. In its 2020 revision of its Code of Ethics, the AIA adopted two new rules: Rule 1.403 against the design of spaces intended for execution, and Rule 1.404 against the design of spaces intended for torture, including indefinite or prolonged solitary confinement. This amendment was a shocking departure for an Institute, which had long resisted calls to limit the role of architects in perpetuating an unjust system of criminal justice. Partners like this and the alternative justice architects, case workers, and advocates at The Spaces of Restorative and Transitional Justice who lend their expertise to the creation of spaces for RJ and TJ work to happen can aid individuals seeking to achieve criminal justice transformation or individual acts of justice.

<u>Use of State Complaint Processes</u>

Change agents must be capable of utilizing existing complaint processes when judges or lawyers engage in misconduct. The Judiciary Commission of Louisiana (JCL) is the body cloaked with authority to evaluate, investigate and make recommendations regarding the misconduct of elected judges and justices of the peace in the state of Louisiana, which involves violations of the Code of Judicial Conduct or the Louisiana Constitution. The JCL can't get involved because a party is not at peace with a decision made by a court. In that instance, the district or appellate courts should be approached. The JCL only has the authority to proceed with complaints that allege things like: (1) willful misconduct relating to official duties; (2) willful and persistent failure to perform duties; (3) persistent and public conduct prejudicial to the administration of justice that brings the judicial office into disrepute; and, (4) conduct while in office which would constitute a felony, or conviction of a felony.

Complaints to the JCL must be submitted in writing, must specifically name a judge or judicial officer (and not name an entire court), and must contain enough specific facts for the JCL to evaluate the judge's alleged conduct. The process begins with an initial screening. If the face of the complaint suggests judicial misconduct is at issue, a response from the judge is solicited and an investigation begins. There could then be a hearing before a hearing officer or the JCL. If discipline is recommended, the matter proceeds to the supreme court for resolution as illustrated:

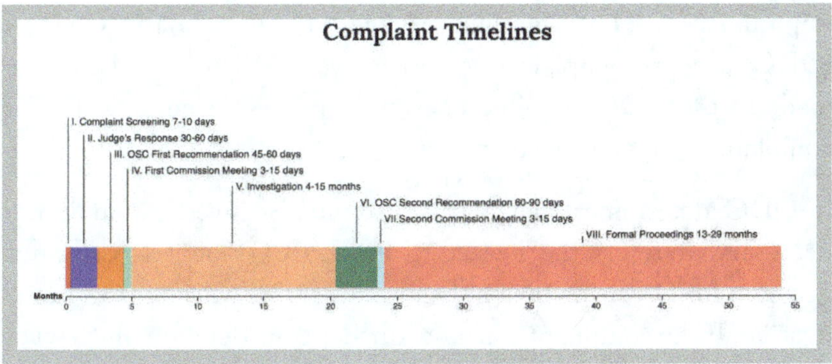

Source: *Judiciary Commission of Louisiana*

Media reporting and public complaints recently led to some changes to the once extreme secrecy that surrounded the process.[93] The new rules say the JCL or a hearing officer may allow judges and other parties involved in a complaint to discuss the proceedings once the commission sets a hearing or when the case is closed.

There is a different process to employ for lawyers accused of breaching their ethical obligations. State and federal courts seemingly espouse the belief that individual prosecutors should continue to be protected by immunity laws. They don't seem to view prosecutorial immunity as necessarily harmful to defendants who can't pursue money damages following the discovery of misconduct. They believe other forms of recourse exist. They see the options–disciplinary action, post conviction relief, sanctions, criminal charges against the prosecutor or using the vote to change D.A.'s–as adequate.[94] They also feel mandatory legal education is sufficient to train and/or punish prosecutors.

After the *Connick v. Thompson* decision (where the SCOTUS found that the municipality was immune from liability for the misconduct of its staff) and the *State v. David Brown* decision (where the court saw no wrong with a prosecutor withholding a confession from the defense because it did not say who did not commit the crime), the lawyer disciplinary process assumes greater importance.[95] The Louisiana Office of Disciplinary Counsel (ODC) accepts complaints against lawyers. When complaints are made to the ODC, a well-orchestrated process is employed. The complaint is first reviewed and screened.

If ODC determines that a full disciplinary investigation is not necessary, it refers the matter to the LSBA Practice Assistance Program for Diversion or simply administratively declines an investigation. If the complaint warrants further consideration, the lawyer is asked to submit a written response to the complaint. During this investigatory stage, facts are gathered to determine whether there is clear and convincing evidence of misconduct on the part of the lawyer. The investigation results in: (1) dismissal; (2) private admonition; and, (3) commencement of formal discipline.

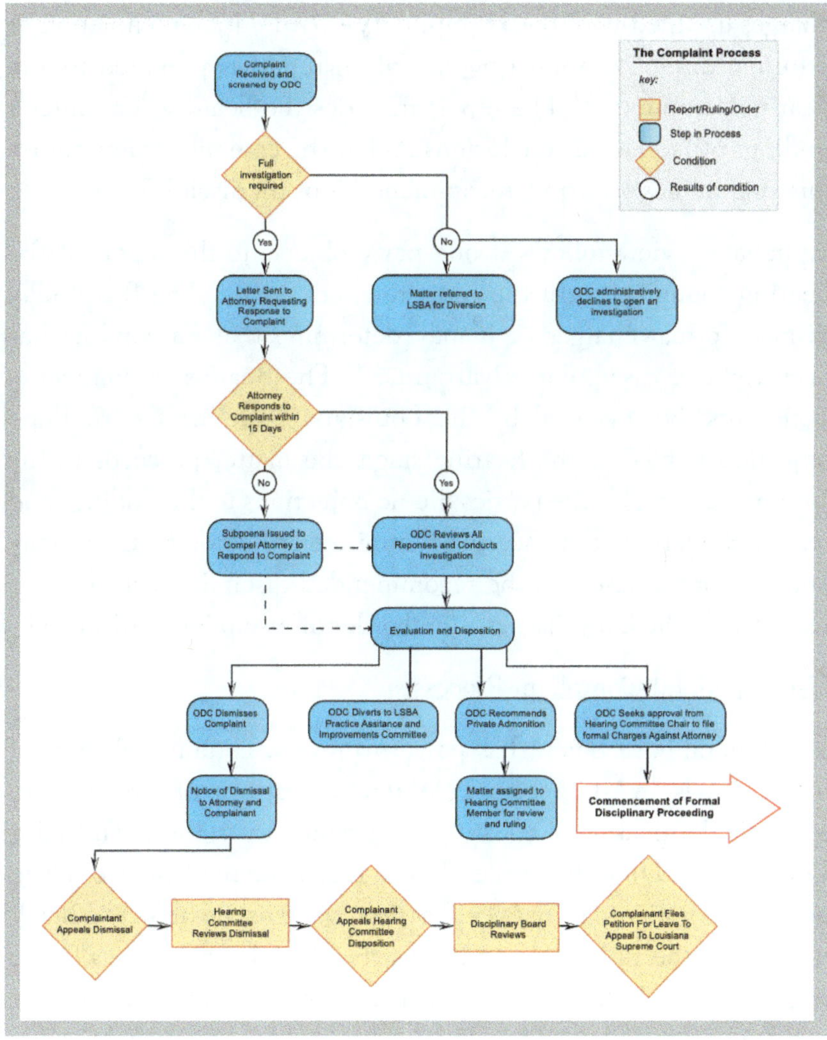

Source: LADB:: Formal Proceedings

Before the ODC can file formal charges, it must receive the permission of a hearing committee chairperson upon a showing of probable cause (that a violation or attempted violation of the Rules of Professional Conduct has occurred or that there are other grounds for lawyer discipline).[96] If the chairperson approves ODC's request, ODC may proceed with the filing of formal charges. The charges are filed with the Disciplinary Board. Upon completion of a formal disciplinary hearing, a written report is prepared by the hearing committee.[97] The report includes the hearing committee's findings of fact, legal conclusions and, if the committee determines misconduct has occurred, recommendations for discipline.

Appellate review follows if one party objects to the report of the hearing committee or if the court remands a case. The Board may dismiss formal charges or it may determine that misconduct has occurred and discipline is warranted.[98] The Board's recommendations must be reviewed by the Louisiana Supreme Court. If no objection is filed at the hearing stage, the matter proceeds to the supreme court.[99] If the parties file no objections to the findings and recommendation of the hearing committee or Board, the Court may enter an order based on the recommended discipline with written reasons.[100] The Court issues a final order of discipline or dismissal.

<u>Use of Federal Complaint Processes</u>

The federal government has power to review certain violations of federal laws by state actors. When a "pattern or practice" or systemic deprivation of constitutional rights exists, the Civil Rights Division (CRD) of the United States Department of Justice (DOJ) has the authority to initiate civil action against state or local officials to remedy the unlawful conditions that impact the masses (not a single person). When the CRD learns of violations of federal criminal law, it has authority to refer incidences to the Criminal Section of the Civil Rights Division. For example, under the Civil Rights of Institutionalized Persons Act ("CRIPA"), 42 U.S.C. § 1997, the Special Litigation Section of the CRD can investigate complaints concerning conditions in state or locally operated prisons, jails, and correctional facilities that affect the masses (not a single person).

The CRD has authority to act on civil rights violations that arise in other contexts. For example, the CRD has used 34 USCA § 12601 (formally 42 U.S.C. § 14141) with some consistency to investigate civil rights violations by law enforcement officers. The CRD also used this same legislation as authority to investigate prosecutors in the Missoula County Attorney's Office in 2012. After seeing this expanded use of § 12601, exoneree John Thompson filed a 2015 complaint to CRD against his prosecutors and the Orleans Parish District Attorney's Office, requesting an investigation and remediation pursuant to § 12601.[101]

John Thompson alleged a pattern and practice in the Orleans Parish D.A.'s office of: (1) *Brady* violations;[102] (2) discrimination against Black jurors; and, (3) prejudicial and improper statements during closing arguments and to the press. Prior to this, a 2013 complaint was made specifically concerning the Angola 3 and generally about the use and abuse of solitary confinement in Louisiana. At that juncture, Herman Wallace and Albert Woodfox had endured over four decades of isolation, believed to be the longest in the state and nation. Change agents should replicate these efforts by utilizing the DOJ's online reporting portal when appropriate.[103]

Use of the United Nations Complaints Process

The educational system in the U.S., even post-secondary institutions, does little to inculcate an awareness of the fact that we, as citizens of the U.S., have protections beyond U.S. law. International human rights law sets forth the obligations of governments to act in certain ways or to refrain from certain acts, in order to promote and protect human rights and fundamental freedoms of individuals or groups.[104] International law, protections and global partners should always be considered when efforts to achieve redress inside the U.S. fail.

There is one illustration worth noting. When we saw Brother John Clutchette was not receiving justice in the U.S. Court system, my students and I sought international protection on his behalf.[105] When we got involved, Clutchette was already in the capable hands of attorney Keith Wattley, a graduate of Santa Clara University School of Law, who operates a law office called UnCommon Law. Wattley is not your typical lawyer. He practices law like the lives of each client is his own. He was giving Clutchette the best quality and effort possible. Because of that, I decided the international lane was the best way to aid the cause.[106]

We considered this matter suitable for their review pursuant to the arbitrary detention mandate by the Special Rapporteur on the Promotion of Truth, Justice, Reparation and Guarantees of Non-Recurrence and by the Special Rapporteur on Minority Issues. We alleged violations of the Universal Declaration of Human Rights (UDHR), the International Convention on Civil and Political Rights (ICCPR) and resolutions calling for processes that aim for truth and justice. As we pursued this international effort in 2017, Whattley continuously litigated the matter in the state of California.

On June 6, 2018, 75-year-old John Clutchette was released from custody. He released a short video extending gratitude for the help.[107] I don't intend to suggest that the international filing caused his release. I do intend to suggest that pressure was built by the collective efforts of myself, my students and Whattley. I also intend to suggest that, often times, our legal system responds better to pressure than truth. The Leonard Peltier and Angola 3 campaigns have also used the U.N. process in conjunction with wrongful detention claims.[108] And, more recently, in 2022, a Louisiana delegate of St. John the Baptist and St. James Parish residents appeared before the Committee on the Elimination of Racial Discrimination in Geneva, Switzerland as it accessed U.S. progress toward ending all forms of discrimination as required by an international treaty passed in 1969.[109]

They provided testimony and called for a moratorium on industrial expansion in Louisiana's "Cancer Alley." They asserted that continuing to build new petrochemical complexes is harmful to neighboring Black communities because of the way they increase pollution. Not long before this, a U.N. appointed special rapporteur called the conditions in the River Parishes "a form of environmental racism" and stated federal regulations failed to protect residents. These strategies work whenever the violation of a human right is at issue and when the U.S has signed an applicable treaty.[110]

To utilize this approach to advocacy, change agents should develop a familiarity with: the Universal Periodic Review, which assesses the fulfillment of member states' human rights obligations; the various treaties and ancillary reporting and complaints processes;[111] public discussion procedure; Special Procedures of the Human Rights Council;[112] the Human Rights Council complaints procedure;[113] and, written communications to committees.[114] Allegations must be substantiated with supporting evidence when that is possible.

<u>Use of Data, Science and Research</u>

I often tell my law students, "in legal writing, your opinion has no value; proof and authority does." It works the same way when it comes to social, law and policy change. Change agents should never expect change solely based on their opinion. Change comes when there is proof and authority to compel it or to silence those who oppose it. Research is very persuasive and it's great authority to use in your quest to either change law or policy, achieve justice or change or oppose change. To be effective with this strategy, change agents must understand how to use research to achieve change.

In instances where changes are pursued extrajudicially, research is as useful as it can be in judicial settings. In 2015, associate professor of history and African-American studies at Valdosta State University Dr. Tom Aiello authored the book, *"Jim Crow's Last*

Stand: Nonunanimous Criminal Jury Verdicts In Louisiana." The original version of the book examines the historical origins of Louisiana's non-unanimous jury law.[115]

As we spoke to elected officials and the community, we used the original version of the book as a complement to the many articles that the advocacy team had authored so there was a range of authority for those seeking quick summaries, to academic journals to those needing detailed explanations.[116] Be cautioned, however. Just having the research is not enough. These two examples illustrate why that is.

When Homer Plessy argued that segregation positions Blacks as inferior beings, the court said if there was a badge of inferiority placed on Blacks, they put it there and not the system of segregation.[117] The court then ruled that segregation did not violate either the Thirteenth or Fourteenth Amendments. The issue was before the SCOTUS again in *Brown v. Board of Education.* Once again, it was argued that segregation caused Blacks to be cast into a position of inferiority. The court agreed this time. What changed? Amongst other social factors, research was used in *Brown.* Black psychologists Mamie and Kenneth Clark's "doll test" study changed the dynamics of the conversation. Dr. Kenneth Clark was the first Black to earn a Ph.D. in psychology at Columbia. His wife Dr. Mamie Clark was the first Black woman and the second Black, after Kenneth Clark, to receive a doctorate in psychology at Columbia.

In their "doll test" study, they used four dolls, identical except for color, to test children's racial perceptions.[118] Their subjects, children between the ages of three to seven, were asked to identify the race of the dolls, which color doll they preferred and which doll was pretty, good and smart. The Black children selected the brown doll when asked which doll looked like them. They selected the white doll in other instances. A majority of the children preferred the white doll and assigned positive characteristics to it. The results served as authority to the *Brown* court–a measure of proof that segregation caused Black children to develop a sense of inferiority.[119]

The use of research as persuasive authority was attempted again when a Black defendant challenged Georgia's capital sentencing scheme as disproportionately subjecting Black defendants who kill white victims to capital sentences. This did not lead to the same success as was achieved in *Brown*. The reason is important to change agents. Mr. McCleskey appealed his conviction and sentence, arguing that the death penalty in Georgia was administered in a racially discriminatory—and therefore unconstitutional–manner. The attorneys couldn't stand before the court and say they should win because it was their opinion there was a racial disparity. As proof, they presented the Baldus study in *McCleskey v. Kemp*.[120]

In this study, Professor David Baldus did a statistical analysis of over 2,000 murder cases in Georgia in the 1970's. The statistics established that, in capital cases, the race of the defendant and victim determined who was sentenced to death. Specifically, Professor Baldus found that Blacks were more likely to receive a death sentence than any other defendants and that Blacks who killed white victims were the most likely to be sentenced to death. His findings indicated that racial bias permeated the Georgia capital punishment system. While the court didn't challenge the results of the study, it didn't find that the study helped on the issue before it so the court ruled that there was no constitutional error.

The court said it needed evidence showing that a specific person in his case acted with a racially discriminatory purpose and not findings about the system in general. I'm not ignoring the outrageous burden of proof created for those seeking to prove discrimination by this case.[121] I'm abstaining from a discussion of it (and how often this happens in law) because the point here is to understand that research alone won't lead to a victory. The research has to speak to the legal standard in place or it has to compel change in an impenetrable way.

McCleskey used this study to support a claim that his Fourteenth Amendment Equal Protection Rights were violated.[122] He claimed, as a Black defendant accused of killing a white victim, the Baldus study demonstrated that he was discriminated against because of his race and because of the race of his victim. Under the long-standing precedent, an allegation such as this requires proof that the purposeful discrimination had a discriminatory effect on the person claiming it. To accomplish this, the mover has to show that those deciding his fate acted with a discriminatory purpose. The court concluded that his proof lacked specificity in that it did not show purposeful actions directed towards him specifically.

Sometimes in the world of social change persuasive speaking skills are sufficient to call people to action, but what happens when people want an independent source for educational or verification purposes? Advocates should always contemplate this moment. If data or research exists, have it ready to share. If it does not, it is your job to facilitate the creation of it. This has happened to me a few times. When I started working on the Angola 3 case, there were news stories and documentaries, but no scholarly sources. I filled that gap by authoring a scholarly law journal article and seeing to it being published.[123] That became an instrument that I used to ignite a national dialogue with other scholars. That prompted speaking invitations and inspired further research surrounding solitary confinement. It was also used when audience members desired a more detailed source or when I was invited to give congressional testimony.

I was confronted with the need for data again when I worked on the campaign to end non-unanimous juries in Louisiana.[124] There was a need to understand how prevalent non-unanimous juries were. The public needed credible answers about the racial implications of these juries relative to both jurors and the accused. Marjorie Esman's decision to invite several members of the media to a panel presentation that the advocacy team organized became the domino that pushed the row down.

It was 2016. It was the first public talk that we did to formally start our campaign to end-non-unanimous juries. At the time, Marjorie was director of the ACLU of Louisiana, a post she held for ten years. Reporters from the Baton Rouge Advocate, the local newspaper, were also in attendance. Not long after, I received this email from a reporter at the Advocate:

Sent: Friday, October 28, 2016 10:39 AM

Hi Angela, I'm the reporter who talked to you last night about pursuing a story about the 10-2 rule in Louisiana. Basically, a small team of us at The Advocate will be working on this for the next few months. I wanted to keep this channel of communication open. Maybe we can get coffee sometime in the next few weeks and chat more about this topic and some ideas you might have about information to look for that would best tell this story. You mentioned you had some information you might be able to send me. Please forward me anything you have on this topic that might be of interest to us, including that Oregon report. The forum last night was very well done, and I appreciate your time.

We had coffee. The end of that meeting became the beginning of The Advocate's investigative series. The world had no clue. The wheels of injustice kept rolling on. It seemed like just another day of the same when New Orleans Criminal District Court Judge Arthur Hunter issued a largely unknown 2017 ruling denying Christopher Lee's motion to declare Louisiana's non-unanimous jury law unconstitutional. Orleans Public Defenders Colin Reingold and Sara O'Brien led the team who claimed that Lee's constitutional rights under the Fourteenth Amendment's Equal Protection Clause were violated by Louisiana's use of non-unanimous juries.

To meet his burden of showing: (1) a discriminatory motive on the part of the legislature; and, (2) a racially disproportionate impact of the law, the defense employed retired Tulane University history professor Dr. Lawrence Powell to discuss the discriminatory motive behind the legislation. In its ruling against Lee, the court explained the need for "direct evidence such as a memo, a quote during the debates, a previous version of the law...which spells out the racial intent." "Dr. Powell's testimony, while compelling, unfortunately does not provide this smoking gun," said the court. Professor Kim Taylor-Thompson, J.D., a professor of Clinical Law at the New York University School of Law testified as to the disproportionate impact of the law, by showing the unreliability of many non-unanimous jury verdicts.

Her testimony was also deemed less than adequate. The court reasoned that it needed to see a statistician or social scientist testify as to the results of a peer-reviewed study, which looked at new data concerning non-unanimous jury verdicts. The court further explained that this data would have been divided based on unanimous and non-unanimous juries and analyzed for guilty, not guilty, hung juries and overturned verdicts and teased apart based on race, gender, and even religion.

The court lamented that "such a study has not been placed before" it and that "isolated cases and journal speculation is not enough to show the court that a racial disparity exists." In discussing the Lee trial strategy many months prior to this dreadful ruling, I sent this email, having no idea when I wrote these closing remarks that a golden egg would soon be laid.

I left home thinking Thursday, March 8, 2018, would be a normal day of "teaching while Black."[125] When I finished my lecture, I returned to an unexpected and astonishing email from a staff member at The Advocate. Included was a summary of the findings of their research that examined various aspects of Louisiana's non-unanimous jury system.[126] Not only did the email contain findings that had never before been attained, but it also contained findings that revealed a system that was far more faulty and far-reaching than even I had imagined. That email did more than validate my personal crusade. It also readied the *Lee* trial team's loss for an impeding conversion to a victory. This is a point to arrest. Change agents should know that the advent of research can sometimes turn a defeat into a delayed victory. The detailed *Lee* opinion became a winning lottery ticket for the *State v. Melvin Maxie* litigation team.[127]

Maxie's lawyers at the Louisiana Capital Assistance Center (LCAC) filed a challenge to the constitutionality of Louisiana's non-unanimous jury law. In the 2018 *Maxie* proceedings, the court conducted a full evidentiary hearing. Attorneys for the state (who have since been promoted to even higher governmental positions) argued in favor of the non-unanimous jury law. They contended that the racist intentions behind the passage of the law faded with time. The state did not call any witness at the hearing on the issue of the constitutionality of Louisiana's non-unanimous jury law. LCAC offered witnesses and exhibits.[128] In *Maxie*, the parties stipulated to a certified transcript of the *State v. Lee* hearing.

LCAC added three live witnesses in addition to this: John Simerman of The Advocate newspaper; Professor Thomas Aiello; and, a second professor whose identity is momentarily withheld. Simerman testified as to the methodology of the study. He also verified and authenticated the data and conclusions as detailed in the published series. Simerman provided a detailed analysis of the collection methods for the dataset used to calculate the impact of non-unanimous juries on Louisiana's criminal legal system. Professor Aiello was accepted by the court as an expert historian. Professor Aiello spoke of racism during and after Reconstruction and the impact it had on Black jury participation, as well as the historical context surrounding the constitutional conventions of both 1898 and 1973.

His testimony persuasively demonstrated that race was a motivating factor behind the adoption of the 1898 constitution, especially with respect to disenfranchisement of minority voters and crippling the ability of minorities to influence judicial outcomes. His testimony also persuasively showed that the 1973 convention was not free from racial considerations and that the delegates at the convention were keenly aware of the racial tensions when drafting the new constitution. His testimony provided the historical basis for this court's determination that the non-unanimous jury verdict scheme in Louisiana was motivated by invidious racial discrimination.

The unnamed professor was accepted by the court as an expert witness with a specialty in legal history, race, and the law. This expert endorsed Professor Aiello's testimony and concurred with his conclusions and analysis. The unnamed professor performed an independent empirical analysis of the data collected by Simerman for *The Advocate's* series. He performed his own data analysis to verify that the results, as presented, were accurate. He also performed an empirical analysis of the disparate impact and racial discrimination data.

The professor explained that he performed his analysis in the context of the literature pioneered by Dr. Kim Taylor-Thompson on "empty votes." The professor also examined the data with respect to the impact on the defendant. He explained that the data revealed that Black defendants were convicted by non-unanimous juries 43 percent of the time and that white defendants were convicted by non-unanimous juries 33 percent of the time. Comparing these rates of conviction by non-unanimous jury verdicts, the anonymous professor found a disparity of approximately 30 percent. That is, Blacks were 30 percent more likely to be convicted by non-unanimous juries than white defendants.

In October 2018, just before Louisiana voters rejected non-unanimous jury verdicts at the polls, Sabine Parish District Judge Stephen Beasley ruled in *Maxie* that non-unanimous jury verdicts were unconstitutional. It was the post-*Lee* research that led to the successful outcome in *Maxie*. This discussion should serve to provide and answer to anyone wondering what to do when data is needed, but lacking. Our system does not accept responsibility for much of what it causes. Change agents have to find ways to get the data or partner with others with the wherewithal to do so.

<u>Being Willing to Aid Others</u>

The work of social change is time-consuming and emotionally exhausting. When you are in the throes of it, it's easy to become too busy to assist some random person, especially since that often means neglecting something that's important to you. It is wise to make careful decisions about the number of things and people one commits to, but I discourage having a default setting of no. The following experiences evidence why.

During the non-unanimous jury campaign, this email came from a person I had never met or heard of. At a time when I was struggling to balance the demands of full-time teaching and research; the pressures of being a spouse, mother and pet owner; and, a volunteer activist:[129]

> Sat 4/21/2018 12:04 PM
>
> Dear Prof. Allen-Bell:
>
> I hope this email finds you well. I'm writing because I am a big fan of your scholarship, and it largely inspired my most recent article, which attempts to build off your "Person of Interest" piece by more closely examining the history of racial discrimination in jury selection throughout the South in the 1880s and 1890s...I would very much love to get your thoughts...

I agreed to review the article, which expanded on the existing scholarship surrounding race and juries. The *Jim Crow Jury* was amazingly well-written so my feedback was minimal. As I read, I learned so, in the end, the benefit was mutual. It was later published in a highly regarded journal. I filed this away as a good deed. In a matter of months, that proved to be an understatement. The author of this article is the unnamed professor I mentioned in the prior discission. At the time, Professor Thomas Frampton was a lecturer at Harvard University. His article *Jim Crow Juries* contributed to Frampton being proffered and accepted by the *Maxie* court as an expert witness with a specialty in legal history, race, and the law. Frampton's work and testimony would again be relied upon during the previously mentioned *Ramos* litigation (where the SCOTUS declared non-unanimous juries in criminal cases unconstitutional).

Another serendipitous email came from an unfamiliar sender after the law changed. It involved the military's use of non-unanimous verdicts as outlined in the Uniform Code of Military Justice. It read:

> Dear Professor Allen-Bell,
>
> I am a military lawyer…Thank you so much for that article. I have used the arguments you presented there to push colleagues in the service, and in Congressional staff offices, to make change.
>
> Efforts to persuade policy makers has met with some limited success…Congress to raise the quorum required for a conviction from 2/3 to 3/4 and to increase the size of General courts-martial from 5 members to 8. Congress enacted those modifications in 2019. But, still, efforts to require unanimity have thus far failed to yield fruit.

> This concerns me greatly. It is especially
> concerning given the way, as your article
> explained, non-unanimous verdicts serve
> to dilute the voice, and thereby
> marginalize, people of color and other
> communities that might offer diverse
> viewpoints during deliberations....

After the 2020 *Ramos* ruling, in July 2021, the Senate Armed Services Committee decided that it was time for the Secretary of Defense to evaluate whether it violates the Constitution to continue allowing non-unanimous juries in court-martial convictions.[130] The senate requested a briefing as to whether *Ramos* should prompt a change of practice.[131] In January of 2022, shock waves were felt amongst the military community. In the case of Lt. Col. Andrew Dial, who was charged with three counts of sexual assault, Judge Col. Charles Pritchard agreed with a defense motion and issued a pretrial ruling requiring, to avoid constitutional shortcomings, a unanimous verdict.

The ruling rested upon the view that non-unanimous jury verdicts infringe on the accused person's Fifth Amendment rights to equal protection. The court found there was no rational basis for Congress to treat service members differently than civilians on this issue. This was unprecedented and it inspired stays in other cases. The trial was paused pending an appeal.[132] The traction in military courts led to scholarly writings in specialized journals that could inform changes in the military. Captain Nino C. Monea's article, *Reforming Military Juries in the Wake of Ramos v. Louisiana* stands out as one.

In the article, the Captain argues that military members are most in need of the protections that a unanimous jury offers because they don't have many of the procedural and constitutional protections that civilians do.[133] Captain Monea refutes the military's position that civilian science research on juries is totally inapplicable to military trials. An unexpected outcome came from the U.S. Court of Appeals for the Armed Forces in July 2023. It concluded that provisions of the Constitution related to Due Process, Equal Protection and unanimous jury verdicts don't invalidate non-unanimous jury verdicts in military courts. As with the *Lee* and *Ramos* rulings, change agents should interpret this as a delay and not a defeat.

The effort even spilled over to Puerto Rico and the United Kingdom. Puerto Rico's Constitution allows non-unanimous jury verdicts in criminal cases with a majority of at least nine jurors. Puerto Rico officials joined the chorus of non-unanimous jury responses by filing briefs with the SCOTUS to announce concerns about the way the *Ramos* decision could affect their convictions.

In 2022, APPEAL, a charity and law practice that provides criminal defense services in England and Wales, launched a research project, *Non-Unanimous Jury Verdicts and Racial Justice*, to explore the potential connection between non-unanimous jury verdicts, race, and miscarriages of justice in England and Wales.

From the initial non-unanimous jury advocacy team, myself and Calvin Duncan were invited to join and serve on an international advisory board along with criminal barristers, academics and the wrongfully convicted.

Angela A. Allen-Bell at the May 2024 APPEAL launch at City Law School in London. Photo credit David Bell.

That effort culminated into a 2024 public report and campaign launch at the City University Law School in London. Efforts to end unanimous-juries there are ongoing.

Co-authors of Doubt Dismissed: Race, Juries and Wrongful Conviction *Nisha Waller & Niama Sakande*

This commitment to never being too busy to assist others was a part of my advocacy approach during my Angola 3 days when this unanticipated email from a congressional staffer arrived:

> Sent: Thursday, February 20, 2014
> 9:34 AM
>
> To: Angela Bell
>
> Subject: Solitary Confinement Hearing
>
> Hi Professor Allen-Bell,

> I hope you are well. Last week, Senator Durbin announced he is holding a follow-up hearing on solitary confinement….We greatly appreciated your submission of written testimony for the June 2012 solitary hearing, and we wanted to reach out and ask you to consider submitting a statement for this hearing as well…

> We also wanted to invite you to attend the hearing….

> Thank you,

I honored this request. What resulted when Senator Dick Durbin, as Chairman of the Senate Subcommittee on the Constitution, Civil Rights, and Human Rights, convened the *Reassessing Solitary Confinement II: The Human Rights, Fiscal, and Public Safety Consequences*, hearing before the Senate Judiciary Subcommittee on the Constitution, Civil Rights, and Human Rights, exceeded the scope of what I could envision at the time.

Those hearings prompted action, largely because of the number of voices, the depth of their knowledge and ranges of their connection to the issue. In January 2016, the DOJ announced the results of a review of the use of restrictive housing in American prisons. The study concluded that there are occasions when correctional officials have no choice but to segregate inmates from the general population, typically when it is the only way to ensure the safety of inmates, staff and the public.

But as a matter of policy, the study noted that this practice should be used rarely, applied fairly and subjected to reasonable constraints. Significantly, the report includes a series of "Guiding Principles" for limiting the use of restrictive housing across the American criminal justice system, as well as specific policy changes that the Bureau of Prisons (BOP) and other DOJ components could undertake to implement these principles.

Since the report was issued, the BOP adopted the majority of the recommendations and continues to take steps to implement them, as well as help ensure that inmates are housed in the least restrictive setting necessary to ensure their own safety and the safety of staff, other inmates and the public. As we are witnessing with state legislation involving divisive concepts and/or critical race theory, a federal position often inspires states to act.[134] So, as I aided in this federal effort, I simultaneously created a basis for state-level reforms.

These examples serve as a reminder that, in the world of social change where agents are always overextended, there will never be a good time to stop and take on more. Inflexibility in these circumstances can cost more time than the pause that assistance requires because, in the end, that very assistance might shorten the life span of your struggle. Change agents must recognize when to extend help and when declining is a better use of your time.

<u>Understanding Timing</u>

Impulse and advocacy do not mix. Advocacy efforts should be carefully timed. Before starting, change agents should pay attention to research, data and best practices. Do they exist? Do they align with your position? Change agents should consult industry standards, best practices, rules, laws, precedents, public policy and regulations. Do they exist? Do they align with your position? Change agents should identify who has the power to give them what they want. Is that person approaching an end of a term of service? Are they new to the office and feeling the need to make a name for themselves? Consideration should be given to the status of the matter at the legislature or in the courts. Is legislation or a ruling on the horizon? Advocates must be mindful of other issues that are consuming the attention of the public and/or elected officials, such as natural disasters. Change agents should be certain that lesser efforts have all been exhausted. Advocates must gauge national traction on their issue. Is there a move around the country to do what you want done? They must also be certain that they have the emotional, physical, financial and logistical capacity to endure an indefinite commitment. Advocacy work should not start before all these things have been considered and all other prerequisites are mastered.

Respecting the Need for Self-Care

The world of change requires the change agent to witness people at their worst on a regular basis. It requires them to ingest suffering, breathe trauma and exhale hurt constantly. Existing in this state produces stress, anxiety and trauma. Chronic stress affects all systems of the body including the musculoskeletal, respiratory, cardiovascular, endocrine, gastrointestinal, nervous, and reproductive systems. Change agents should also understand that stress can be passed from person-to-person. An excessive or persistent state of anxiety also has a devastating effect on physical and mental health because of the way it increases breathing and heart rate. Trauma harms the body to such a dangerous degree that it can actually impact brain functioning and alter behavior.

Change agents can also fall victim to second-hand stress, which is passed through facial expressions, voice frequency, odor and touch. Change agents must adopt strategies for managing trauma, stress and anxiety, such as maintaining a healthy social support network, getting an adequate amount of sleep each night, becoming self-protective of your energy, meditation, setting boundaries between work and rest, having regular escapes from stress, breathing and physical exercises. I recently adopted what has now become my favorite technique: intentional rest and repose.

CHAPTER 2
ADVOCACY STRATEGIES

Each day, I feel less like a lawyer and more like a part of a modern Underground Railroad System. My work involves the daily disruption of a state-sanctioned human trafficking system and the battling of Jim Crow who refuses to be evicted from the South.

— ANGELA A. ALLEN-BELL

I have been a licensed attorney in the state of Louisiana for nearly thirty years. My tryst with the legal system has caused me to see its shortcomings and our overreliance on it. I am not opposed to civil litigation or criminal prosecutions. Many major milestones have been accomplished through civil litigation and public safety demands a means to hold people accountable for breaking laws. I do, however, oppose overdependence on the judiciary, trust in a system that has not earned it, naivety when it comes to a legal system that is as fractured and damaged as the one I have come to know in Louisiana and a blind belief that litigation alone works in all cases. Sometimes advocacy should be an alternative to litigation.

Other times, advocacy must be used in conjunction with litigation. Change agents must understand the way these forces work in sync to achieve justice, change and /or long-term transition from systems that harm.

A range of templates for successful social change exists. The *Comité des Citoyens* (Citizens Committee in English), a group that existed during the lynching era, gave us a very useful model to consider as a starting point. These Black business and thought-leaders, who opposed segregation in the 1880's used a three-pronged approach to social change: (1) litigation; (2) direct action (such as strikes, protests or onsite challenges to a law); and, (3) public education and publicity campaigns (such as use of print media). The Citizens Committee strategy was adopted by the NAACP and was used by those of us who did the work of ending non-unanimous juries in Louisiana.

The Black Panther Party (BPP) is another example to consider. Community education and empowerment were trademarks of the BPP. The Louisiana BPP chapter fed children; operated a liberation school for youth; provided security and protection to the community; engaged in crime prevention; assisted the elderly as their needs dictated; held community and political education and self-determination classes; provided pest control, tutoring and transportation services; provided sickle cell screenings and security to residents; organized neighborhood cleanups; established a drug-free zone and offered drug treatment; visited and supported incarcerated BPP members; maintained a heaqquarters and saw to associated administrative tasks; solicted food to give away or prepare; and, raised funds in order to sustain their efforts.

BPP chapters labored without a salary from early morning until night. The areas that the BPP lived and worked in were dilapidated and crime-infested. In one instance, New Orleans officials acknowledged the city's refusal to serve jury summons' to residents of the Desire Housing Project (Desire) and conceded they undertook this unconstitutional act for safety reasons. At this same time, the BPP volunteered to live and work in the Desire because service was their love language to Black people. Before their arrival, the areas they served were crime and drug-infested and residents of these communities were hopelessly disconnected from city services and the democracy, in general. The Louisiana chapter nearly eradicated despair, violence and crime in the area surrounding the Desire.

Angela A. Allen-Bell, Noel Dauzart, Dr. Clyde Robertson & Tiffany Rainey with members of
Louisiana's BPP chapters (both the Angola chapter & the New Orleans chapter) in 2020.
Photo credit Darlene Holmes.

Had the chapter not been neutralized, I am certain that people of color in Louisiana would have lower rates of divorce, incarceration and crime and higher rates of literacy and economic prowess. On a national level, the BPP's political lobbying led to passage of the Sickle Cell Act and President Richard Nixon's mention of sickle cell for the first time in a State of the Union address. The award-winning community school that they operated in California was so successful that, in 1977, the California State Legislature issued a commendation to the Oakland Community Learning Center "for having set the standard for the highest level of education in the state." The BPP's work in inspiring Black children to become educated and disciplined is unmatched. While the BPP's organizational life span lasted sixteen years, their contribution to America continues.

A Citizens' Complaint Board to hear allegations of police abuse was established by the Oakland City Council in 1981, fourteen years after the BPP launched its community patrols of the police. This model has been replicated and reused. They taught us how to effectively use multicultural alliances. Their emphasis on community-based initiatives laid the foundation for many modern social justice movements. Their breakfast program and food give aways raised public consciousness about hunger and poverty in the United States and became a precursor to the present free school lunch programs that we have all come to know. Their efforts where Sickle Cell Anemia is concerned laid the groundwork for our current medical awareness and response.

Art and message from Angola 3 & BPP member Herman Wallace to Angela A. Allen-Bell.

BPP activism provides a model of community self-help. When the BPP spoke of a revolution in speeches and in their newspaper, they were speaking of a revolution of the people. They felt the education they were teaching the people would cause the people to rise up—not through violence, but through action—through democratic participation. They wanted revolution through office holding and voting. They saw that as a pathway to equality. Co-founder Bobby Seale explained it this way: "Revolution is about re-evolving... putting political, economic and social power back in the hands of the people." They had their own unique approach to social change. It was highly successful.

Dr. Gail Christopher is the architect of the Truth, Racial Healing & Transformation (TRHT) approach to social change. The TRHT is an adaptation of the internationally recognized Truth and Reconciliation Commission (TRC) model, which has been instrumental in resolving deeply rooted conflicts around the world. TRHT helps communities across the U.S. embrace racial healing and uproot the conscious and unconscious belief in a hierarchy of human value that limits equal access to quality education, fulfilling employment, safe neighborhoods, equal housing opportunities, quality health-care and equitable treatment of all people. Through work under the pillars illustrated below, TRHT engages communities in racial healing and equity work:

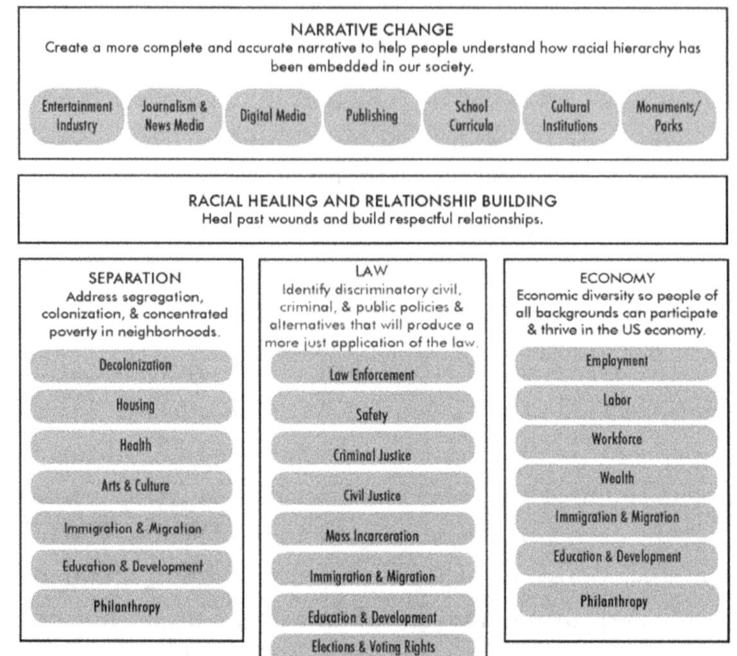

Through truth and recognition of history, the TRHT approach leads to equitable policy solutions and new ways of relating as human beings. The TRHT offers specific guidance when it comes to law. It calls upon the nation to recognize the way our system of law has perpetuated the hierarchy of human value. Accordingly, TRTH "embraces a system of law that reflects our common humanity, the dignity of all people and our commitment to the civil and human rights of all. [It] seeks to redress the inequities in our legal system that have been created by the belief in a hierarchy of human value...[a]nd [calls for] full civic participation in our nation and in our communities."

My book *Diversity in the Jury Box and Beyond: A Formula for Transforming Louisiana Injustice System* takes inspiration from these models. I, ultimately, unveil a two-part process for transforming Louisiana's legal system or any other racialized social system or system that harms. In that book, I offer deliberative process research as the *means* to achieving individual (micro-level) change and TJ as the *ends* for achieving group (mezzo-level) and governmental (macro-level) change. That deliberative process research teaches that, to serve its tremendous purpose, jury diversity must exist because of the way a range of perspectives improves deliberations.

That deliberate process research also hints to the virtues of equity, inclusion and belonging during the deliberation process (though not described in those exact terms). The deliberative process research teaches that marginalizing one or two jurors is detrimental to an accused person in the same way that a lack of jury diversity is. By extension, marginalizing or excluding individuals in society or operating without diversity, equity, inclusion and belonging is as harmful to a society as it is to an accused person whose fate rests in the hands of a jury. After individual (micro-level) change is underway, *Diversity in the Jury Box and Beyond,* shifts focus to achieving group (mezzo-level) and governmental (macro-level) change through the pillars of TJ.

TJ aims to both redress legacies of atrocities and to promote long-term, sustainable peace. TJ emerged as part of a recognition that dealing with systematic or massive abuses requires a distinctive approach that is both backward and forward looking; that dignifies victims, but prevents similar victimhood in the future. The long-term goals of TJ measures are to promote peace, democracy and reconciliation, with the idea that these conditions help to prevent systematic or massive violations of human rights.

TJ employs a "range of processes and mechanisms associated with a society's attempt to come to terms with a legacy of large-scale past abuses, in order to ensure accountability, serve justice, provide remedies to victims, promote healing and reconciliation, enhance equity, inclusion and belonging, establish independent oversight of the security system, restore confidence in the institutions of the state and promote the rule of law."[1] TJ primarily seeks to change how citizens interact with one another and with state officials, to reduce structural inequality and to eliminate normalized wrongdoing. There are five pillars of a TJ model: (1) truth-seeking; (2) memorialization; (3) prosecutions/justice; (4) reparations; and, (5) legal and policy reforms/the guarantee of non-recurrence.

The work of social change is not a rigid science and it rarely relies on a single action.[2] What's more likely is a long-lasting effort that involves many actions. For purposes of inspiration, let's consider some of the various things one can do to achieve justice and/or transition.

<u>Using Litigation</u>

In 2018, after the unanimous jury campaign ended, the SCOTUS agreed to hear *Ramos v. Louisiana*, a case involving a man sentenced to life without parole despite two of his twelve jurors voting against convicting. Attorney Ben Cohen adoringly reflected, "Calvin Duncan was my partner in this. Whenever I was too tired to go on, he would carry me. And we would think about new ways to challenge the legality of the rule." The pair's persistence paid off.

Ramos determined whether the Sixth Amendment right to a jury trial—as incorporated against the states by way of the Fourteenth Amendment—requires a unanimous verdict to convict a defendant of a serious offense in state court. In April 2020, the SCOTUS set aside years of precedent and declared that unanimous juries are a constitutional requirement.[3] Tragically, further litigation needed to be pursued. By the time of the *Ramos* ruling, Thedrick Edwards' conviction from thirteen years prior had become final and his appeal rights had been exhausted. On one charge, Thedrick was convicted by a 10-2 verdict and, on the other, he was convicted by a 11-1 verdict.

In *Edwards v. Vannoy*, Thedrick's attorney André Bélanger, began his argument to the SCOTUS with a reminder of what the SCOTUS said when they decided *Ramos*. "A verdict of eleven is no verdict at all," said Bélanger before he asked if the rule from *Ramos* applied retroactively so people like Thedrick, who had what *Ramos* deemed unconstitutional trials, could receive a constitutional process. In a May 2021 opinion, the SCOTUS answered in the negative, holding that the *Ramos* ruling did not apply retroactively on *federal* collateral review.[4] The SCOTUS did note that states remained free to apply the jury-unanimity rule retroactively in state, post-conviction proceedings if it so desired.

The latter pronouncement prompted even more litigation. In May 2022, *Reddick v. Louisiana* was argued before the Louisiana Supreme Court after the attorney general challenged a district court decision granting a new trial when a judge ruled that Reddick's original non-unanimous jury conviction was unconstitutional. In his case, there was no physical evidence and only testimony of one witness whose statements changed four times between the day after the crime and Reddick's trial. Reddick was convicted despite two jurors raising reasonable doubt and voting against a conviction.

Reddick asked the Louisiana Supreme Court if those with final convictions at the time of the *Ramos* ruling had a right to a new trial. The fate of around 1,500 people who remained incarcerated with non-unanimous jury verdicts rested in the hands of the justices. The court denied relief because of the "strong reliance interests at stake and the high administrative burden that many retrials of final convictions would impose...."[5] In response, Judge Piper Griffin did what Xavier Prep women do.[6] Through her audacious dissent, she spoke truth, demonstrated empathy and urged accountability:

> Unanimous jury verdicts are so fundamental to due process and fairness that the people of Louisiana amended their Declaration of Rights. If the right is necessary for procedural fairness for future cases, it is also necessary for past cases.... Intentional racism has no place in our criminal justice system....The racially discriminatory nature of convictions secured by non-unanimous verdicts does not change over time. Such convictions were racially discriminatory in 1898. They were racially discriminatory in 1975. They remain racially discriminatory today. The imperative to correct past injustices manifests in the deprivation of a constitutionally guaranteed right should not cede to reliance interests and administrative concerns. Rather, 'it is a cost we must bear if we mean to show that we guarantee all Louisianans equal justice.'[7]

Justice James T. Genovese penned a vigorous partial dissent:

> I find...only those defendants who were convicted by non-unanimous verdicts due to racial animus are entitled to relief on collateral review....a non-unanimous jury verdict without racial animus would not qualify for relief on collateral review....racial animus is present when the jury vote of an African American is disenfranchised and discounted, which occurs when a jury can reach a verdict without said African American vote under the prior non-unanimous verdict rule of law....[8]

This summary reveals that it can sometimes take multiple suits, over many years, to accomplish one change. Other times, a single suit can accomplish justice. Through this example, change agents should also see how litigation can also serve as work under the truth-seeking and memorialization pillars. It can even lay the groundwork for reparations, prosecutions or legal reforms. This happened in the case of BPP member Fred Hampton. It also happened in the case of Martin Luther King. Both cases unearth the truth and provided a written record of the harms done at the urging of official actors. Sometimes ancillary efforts must be pursued in conjunction with litigation or as an alternative to it. Let's consider some ways direct action can be used towards these ends.

<u>Use of Public Spaces</u>

The relationship between democracy and public spaces is undeniable. The aims of a democracy are satisfied when there is public discourse, debate and discussion about matters of concern to the collective. The First Amendment is considered a layer of protection against this precious right ever being lost or encroached upon. Amongst other things, this amendment grants freedom of speech, the right of the people to peaceably assemble and petition the government for redress of grievances.[9]

When it comes to Blacks, Louisiana has always been resistant to group gatherings and opposed to certain messages reaching Black ears. From the point that Blacks were trafficked into the state to be enslaved, both have been outlawed. In 1851, Michael Read was prosecuted for making these public remarks in West Feliciana parish:

> The negroes (meaning the slaves of the parish and State aforesaid) are as free as the white men (meaning the white men of the parish and State aforesaid.) This is a free country, (meaning the parish and State aforesaid,) and that the negroes (meaning the slaves of and in said parish and State) have no right to call any man master.[10]

The state accused Read of using language that had a tendency to produce discontent among the free colored population and to excite insubordination among the slaves. For these remarks, Read was found guilty and sentenced to five years at hard labor in the state penitentiary. It did not matter that the First Amendment was adopted in 1791, sixty years *prior to* this. The historical remnants of this fear of Black dissent, protest and activism remain. Despite Emancipation and the Reconstruction era amendments extending constitutional protections to Blacks, change agents should always consider this when speech or assembly involves persons of color.

Change agents should also understand the intended limits of the First Amendment. While the First Amendment does envision advocacy, assembly and demonstrations, it does not protect acts of terrorism, violence or incitement to imminent violence. Those are all considered unprotected criminal acts. Advocates must understand that First Amendment rights are not absolute. Certain regulations on time, place and manner of speech can be imposed when certain governmental interests are at stake. Conditions, such as requiring permits and preventing blockage of certain roadways, can be placed upon organizers of public demonstrations. It's also necessary that advocates understand that the First Amendment treats public and private property differently.

Protections are greater the more public a space is. Traditionally, parks, streets and sidewalks have been viewed as public forums. Problems arise because organizers, police and judges don't always agree on what's public or private. The wrong call could result in criminal charges, such as trespassing. Organizers must understand the evolving nature of First Amendment protections and must assume the responsibility for knowing the limits of what is and is not lawful before advocacy in this manner is undertaken. Activists must also understand that laws are not self-executing. People have to interpret and apply them. When a person has power and wishes to use it to silence grievances, the First Amendment won't always stop them immediately, which means activists must sometimes embrace the ancillary duty of becoming a party to a First Amendment challenge.

Louisiana is a case study in First Amendment abuses on the part of state officials. Change agents should understand the nuances of these local cases and use them as planning tools. John Garner and his fellow students took a seat at a segregated lunch counter in Baton Rouge in 1961. They were arrested and charged with the crime of disturbing the peace. On the day in question, the store manager, who was also seated at the lunch counter, instructed the waitress to tell Garner and the other students that they could not be served at the whites-only counter.

She advised them that they could be served if they moved to the counter across the aisle that was reserved for Blacks. They did not move. One placed an order for a beverage. Their presence was deemed a disturbance. They were subsequently convicted. Jail time and a fine was imposed. In *Garner v. Louisiana*, the SCOTUS determined that the students did not conduct themselves in a manner that would foreseeably disturb or alarm the public. Rather, the court found their actions peaceful. The court held that the convictions were devoid of evidentiary support and, therefore, unconstitutional under the Due Process Clause of the Fourteenth Amendment.

The next noteworthy case arises in New Orleans. When the NAACP and older New Orleans activists deemed sit-ins too radical, in the summer of 1960, Oretha Castle Haley, Rudy Lombard and Jerome Smith organized a small cadre of student activists into a Congress of Racial Equality (CORE) chapter. That led to the arrest of three Black and one white student in *Lombard v. Louisiana* after they ignored a restaurant manager's instruction to leave a private New Orleans establishment.

At the time those students sat at a lunch counter (that was not designated for any race), Louisiana law prohibited integration. They were later convicted of criminal mischief, sentenced to jail time and a fine was imposed. A week prior, both the Mayor of New

Orleans and the Superintendent of Police spoke on the issue of activism towards the ends of ending segregation. The police chief said:

> We believe it is most important that the mature responsible citizens of both races...continue the exercise of sound, individual judgment, goodwill and a sense of personal and community responsibility....With the exercise of continued, responsible law-abiding conduct by all persons, we see no reason for any change whatever in the normal, good race-relations that have traditionally existed in New Orleans....We wish to urge the parents of both white and Negro students who participated in today's sit-in demonstration to urge upon these young people that such actions are not in the community interest.[11]

The mayor said:

> I have today directed the superintendent of police that no addi-
> tional sit-in demonstrations or so-called peaceful picketing outside
> retail stores by sit-in demonstrators or their sympathizers will be
> permitted....This is in keeping with the oft-announced policy of
> the New Orleans city government that peace and order in our city
> will be preserved....I have carefully reviewed the reports of these
> two initial demonstrations by a small group of misguided white
> and Negro students, or former students....the effect of such
> demonstrations is not in the public interest of this community.[12]

Once again, the SCOTUS sided with activists against Louisiana officials when it came to the First Amendment. The court did so because the testimony showed that the students did not cause a disturbance and because the state did not meet its burden of proof. The court was not persuaded by attempts on the part of state officials to elevate the authority of the mayor and police chief so as to make their statements have the weight of law. State officials would later denounce CORE as "one of the United States' most subversive organizations."[13]

Astonishingly, a mere two years later, another First Amendment case would make its way to the SCOTUS because of Louisiana officials again attempting to criminalize public dissent. The 1965 case of *Cox v. Louisiana* arose because Black ministers and college students from Southern University (S.U.) had been actively picketing segregated lunch counters in Baton Rouge. Some of them were arrested. The arrested students were held in the parish jail, which was located inside the courthouse. Other students and community members, led by Ronnie Moore, CORE student president, planned to appear in front of the courthouse to protest these arrests and continued segregation.

On the day of the planned gathering, Moore was taken into custody and the CORE Vice President was already in jail so B. Elton Cox, minister, civil rights advocate and CORE field secretary, decided to lead. Cox arrived to approximately 2000 students assembled at the Old State Capitol, which was about two and a half blocks from the courthouse. Rain fell throughout the day. Cox ensured the group was orderly and not blocking traffic or the streets. Cox did not disband the group as requested by the sheriff's department official, but he did explain their intentions, which was to say prayers, sing hymns and conduct a peaceful protest. Cox refused a second request to disband. After traveling a few blocks in an orderly fashion, the group was stopped again and asked by law enforcement to explain the purpose of the gathering. Cox complied.

There is a dispute as to what happens next. Cox says law enforcement instructed him to "confine the demonstration to the west side of the street." According to him, the group moved to the west side of the street and then proceeded (never obstructing the street). Some white onlookers gathered. Cox spoke to the group, emphasizing peace and denouncing violence. After, he said, "let's go eat." In response, the sheriff told the group that things just turned violent and that the group needed to disband. Tear gas followed. The students abandoned the demonstration and fled to safety. Cox was arrested the next day. No others were ever arrested.

Cox was acquitted of criminal conspiracy, but convicted of disturbing the peace, obstructing public passages and picketing after the trial judge equated Black group gatherings with inherently dangerous behavior:

> It must be recognized to be inherently dangerous and a breach of the peace to bring 1,500 people, colored people, down in the predominantly white business district...and congregate across the street from the courthouse and sing songs...carrying lines such as 'black and white together' and to urge those 1,500 people to

descend upon our lunch counters and sit there until they are served.[14]

Jail time and a fine were imposed. The SCOTUS ruled against Louisiana officials again. The court deemed the breach of peace law constitutionally defective and, after viewing the footage, found the actions of the students lawful, peaceful and orderly. Louisiana continued in its wayward ways.

A new reality was ushered in in 1971. That year, the Twenty-Sixth Amendment to the United States Constitution was ratified. It gave 18-year-olds the right to vote. Public protests, challenges and activism were of tremendous concern during this era because of the potential influence they could have on this new, impressionable pool of voters. This presented specific concerns for President Richard M. Nixon as he geared for reelection.

With these precedents set in the 1960s, it would seem Louisiana officials would be unwilling to trample upon protected First Amendment rights anymore. But that is exactly what happened in July 2016 when roughly one hundred and eighty-five protesters were arrested during their non-violent protest of the murder of Alton Sterling, a Baton Rouge citizen who was shot by a member of the Baton Rouge Police Department (BRPD) after being tased and pinned to the ground. Many of these protesters were nonviolent and compliant as they sang, prayed and displayed signs in silence.

A number of lawsuits complained of indiscriminate police brutality and resulting bodily injuries, wrongful arrests, harsh jail conditions, constitutional violations and an ultimate aim to chill protest. The response to these arrests and suits is telling. Charges were dropped and settlements were made in many instances, suggesting, like those exercising First Amendment rights in *Garner, Lombard and Cox*, the citizens had more respect for the rule of law than official actors.[15]

The reporters, students, legal observers and citizens in the *Imani v. City of Baton Rouge* litigation did not settle their cases. They—with the masterful representation of attorneys William Most, David Lanser and John Adcock—accused the police of violating their First, Fourth and Fourteenth Amendment rights of free speech, protection from excessive force and the right to a fair judicial process. They set out at trial to prove the above damning allegations as well as claims that: law enforcement wrote affidavits of probable cause on pre-fabricated forms that included facts from an entirely different event; used forged signatures on warrants; aimed machines guns and assault rifles at nonviolent and compliant protesters; gave conflicting orders to protesters; and, separated families and pets as they made arrests.

I was mortified as I witnessed and read the testimony of some members of law enforcement and observed others invoke the Fifth Amendment (to avoid incriminating themselves). Apparently, city officials were too. The trial was abruptly stopped. The East Baton Rouge Parish City Council swiftly approved a settlement that awarded this group of Sterling protesters $1.17 million dollars.

Change agents must also understand that lead organizers can be targeted. In *Doe v. Mckesson*, a BRPD officer claiming he lost teeth and suffered other injuries during the protests sued DeRay Mckesson and Black Lives Matter, a movement that is not a formal organization. That lawsuit does not accuse Mckesson of injuring the officer. The suit claims the activist "conspired to violate the law by planning to block a public highway" and "incited violence." In March 2022, the Louisiana Supreme Court ruled, purely as a matter of state tort law, that a person can be held liable for negligently precipitating the crime of a third party.

In 2023, the Fifth Circuit, guided by the state court's conclusion that, under state tort law, protest organizers may be held accountable for the actions of those attending a protest, rendered a troubling ruling that threatens all Americans' ability to organize protests. The court found that Mckesson did not throw any objects or cause the injuries in question, but they concluded he was a fault for leading a protest "in front of the Baton Rouge police station" and for attempting "to block a public highway." According to the Fifth Circuit's ruling, a protest organizer who commits even minor legal violations such as these may potentially be held liable for the illegal actions of someone else who attended the protest. Judge Don Willett dissented.

Willett said, "Holding Mckesson responsible for the violent acts of others because he 'negligently' led a protest that carried the risk of potential violence is impossible to square with Supreme Court precedent holding that only tortious activity meant to incite imminent violence, and likely to do so, forfeits constitutional protection against liability for violent acts committed by others." In 2024, the SCOTUS refused to hear the matter. This litigation is part of a larger (and continuous) effort to silence dissent. During the 2022 Regular Session, Republican Danny McCormick introduced legislation to expand Louisiana's justifiable homicide law to include murders "committed for the purpose of preventing imminent destruction of property or imminent threat of tumultuous and violent conduct during a riot." Many exhaled when the bill failed to become law then, in 2024, lawmakers brewed a more lethal dose of legislation.

Governor Landry signed House Bill 173 into law, making it a crime to come within twenty-feet of a police officer upon command. During that same session, lawmakers approved House Bill 127 to establish harsher punishment for anyone who organizes a protest that ends up disrupting traffic and House bill 383, which leaves pedestrians with no course of civil legal action against drivers who injure them during protests if that driver feels threatened. Public spaces are important sites for change agents to work, but they should only be used after a thorough understanding of how to avoid the harms associated with them and after an arrest, bail and legal representation plan has been fortified.

Using Public Education and Publicity Campaigns to Achieve Change

Billboards

Photo Credit Ben Cohen.

Billboards are recommended because of the way they allow communication with busy people who might not ordinarily stop to listen. They are also useful because they reach people on a subconscious level, which means you don't have to do the work of convincing a person to listen. They were used at different intervals during the non-unanimous jury campaign. D.A. DeRosier's comments before the legislature earned him the above billboard. The billboard reads: "What does D.A. John DeRosier think about the origins of a racist law? It is what it is." The below billboard was used after the *Reddick* case was filed with Louisiana's Supreme Court.

Photo credit David Bell.

Posters and Signage

Posters and signage remove many of the challenges that verbal communication poses. You don't have to struggle with tone or approach. You just have to create a jolting and effective way to say what you want heard and you must ensure your message is seen by the right readers. Reverend Anderson and members of EBRPPRC, an organization that formed as a result of the alarming number of deaths of persons inside the East Baton Rouge Parish Prison, regularly utilize this method.

At Metro Council meeting advocating for accountability for the deaths that have occurred in the Baton Rouge jail. Photo credit EBRPPRC.

EBRPPRC Caravan for Justice. Photo credit EBRPPRC.

Press Conferences

Press conferences generate awareness of a cause and "increase media interest in your advocacy initiative and can help you reach your target audiences."[16] "They give you the opportunity to tell the media about major new developments related to your issue, or about special advocacy events that will take place."[17]

When planning a press conference, location and objectives are initial considerations. The press conference should be held near the location of decision makers, near the physical space of challenge or where the greatest number of onlookers can see.

Photos from April 17, 2012 press conference commemorating the 40th anniversary of the Angola 3 being placed in solitary confinement. Held outside the Louisiana State Capitol Building. Photo credit Jackie Sumell.

Organizers should consider applicable regulations, such as permits or insurance. There should be a well-considered objective. Speakers should be carefully planned to lend credibility to the occasion. And it's a good idea to use imagery to lure people into the conversation.

Photo credit Jackie Sumell.

Photo credit Jackie Sumell.

The purpose should remain at the forefront during planning. Organizers should consider if the event is for amplification, education, to secure funding, tied to a specific action item or for no other purpose than to meet the community's need to say, "enough is enough." Rev. Anderson also urges attention to the role you will assume as plans are considered. "Are you the 'expert,' the 'supportive friend,' the survivor,' 'the challenger'," asks Anderson.

<u>Websites</u>

When a person is harmed by the legal system or any system, a website can be a useful organizing and educational tool. They are best used when they include developments, important dates, action calls and resources, such as investigative reports, official decisions and/or evidence. This affords the public an opportunity to study the issue and assist in educated and informed ways. It serves as a tool for organizing a public presence when needed. It also demonstrates a base of support for the person or cause. One of the more frequent requests I get is for insights on websites for use as an advocacy tool on behalf of a justice-impacted victim. There are a few sites to consider. They are:

- Freeleonard.org: For Leonard Peltier
- Angola3.org: For the Angola 3

Websites can also accomplish the purposes of truth-seeking and memorialization, as well as build a case for reparations and policy reforms.

<u>Second Lines</u>

Those in ear shot of the New Orleans Treme Center on October 1, 2014, witnessed the second line being used as a means of public education that could lead to social, legal and policy change. Spectators were roused by the sounds of the Free Spirit Brass Band and the Solider Brass Band as they performed at the second line for

Angola 3 member Albert Woodfox. By its very nature, a second line inspires participation.

Second lines cast a spell of jubilation over onlookers and participants, but they have utility beyond beguilement. An examination of the origins of second lines, which are derived from African tribal customs, reveals earnest purposes. Like all else in Louisiana, race governed the sale of insurance, financial services and burials post-slavery. Black benevolent organizations developed in the 1800s to meet this need. Blacks paid membership dues to these societies and, in turn, could depend on funds needed to cover health care expenses, burials or other financial hardships.

One example is the New Orleans Freedmen's Aid Association, founded in 1865 at the end of the Civil War to provide loans and education to newly freed people. To advertise or thank the community for patronizing them, these organizations hosted neighborhood celebrations. Modern second lines morphed from this. The second line tradition evolved to include celebrations of both life and death.

<u>Using the Arts</u>

When I studied human rights as a law student, I was shocked to learn that art is one of the thirty recognized human rights.[18] The seed that was planted while I was a law student blossomed about fifteen years into my career as a lawyer when I had an epiphany. It dawned on me that, if art needed this level of protection, there must have been forces interested in silencing certain messages and, when there is a will to silence, there is an awareness of the impact of speech. With this understanding, art, a form of speech and expression, became a resource I look to for achieving social change.

Art can promote a deeper understanding of our shared humanity. Art can elevate and amplify the voices of those most affected by injustice. It can inspire community support and it can empower and educate those in power. Art can create inclusive dialogues that allow members of marginalized groups to be heard. It can help people identify and empathize with the experiences of others. Art can teach the younger generation about a past they did not live and aid in exploring causes of past and present injustices. Below are a few ways you might use art to educate about needed social, legal or policy changes.

Plays

Producer and playwright Parnell Herbert, part of the Angola 3 advocacy team, brainstormed for ways to aid in the release of the Angola 3 and, in the process, educate about the harms of solitary confinement. Having great success with a prior production, he settled upon a play. I had the honor of being in the audience to witness his impactful stage play, *Angola 3*. His play placed the audience in the distressing company of evil and forced the audience to do the loathsome work of examining souls.

He cleverly littered the script with laughs, which strategically disrupted paralyzing anguish and tribulation. The play managed to take the audience many places and returned them forever changed. The cast did not act; they owned the characters. Herbert, a U.S. Navy veteran, staged this play in multiple venues and in multiple states over a ten-year span. When he wrote his first play, his only experience was the chuckle-packed stories he wrote to himself as a child and a stint as an unofficial ghostwriter for his fellow sailors who requested poems and letters to wives and sweethearts.

Photo credit Parnell Herbert.

Herbert urges advocates to consider this form of advocacy, either directly or through partnerships with playwrights, because of the far reach plays can have and because of the unique way they can inspire action. But he warns, "a play is not a magic bullet; it's a tool that allows change agents to meet people where they are." He continued, "the public often wants to do something to cause change, but are sometimes unsure of what they can do." This is because, he explained, "they are unaware of the power of a united people."

After some performances, audience members asked what they could do to help. Herbert always suggested they look within by reflecting on the resources, skills and natural assets they had to aid movements for change and transformation. He also boasts of the utility of question-answer sessions at the end of performances and he insists on always preparing a few demands to share with the audience as a "call to action."

Photo credit Parnell Herbert.

I asked Herbert how he knew the play helped the cause. He reported noticing more dialogue and debate about solitary confinement, greater public presence for subsequent court proceedings, greater media coverage and increased attention to the case by other artists, such as one being called to paint a massive mural.

Artist Brandon "B Mike" Odums and others. Photo credit Parnell Herbert.

He refused to say the Angola 3 play ignited the blaze, but he's sure the play, and each other advocacy attempt, added a bit of fuel to the flames. In time, it ignited. He sees his advocacy work as a continuation of the type of service to his country that he started as a young sailor. The release of these men competes with the pride he feels about his military service. "Herman and Albert left those prison grounds in an ambulance, not a hearse; not as a dead convict, but as a newly freed citizen." He continued, "Robert is now living the free life he deserves and, just as an old Backwoods warden who fled his post under a cloud of suspicion once said, he is still practicing BLACK PANTHERISM. POWER TO THE PEOPLE!!!"

<u>Cinema/Film</u>

Fate led Ben Donnellon, who earned a B.S. in Cinema and Photography from Ithaca College in New York and a Master of Fine Arts in Film from the University of New Orleans, to read a 2016 news-paper article about Louisiana's non-unanimous jury system shortly after he moved to Louisiana. Outrage over what he read prompted him to contact one of the cited sources. Before long, Ben Donnellon and his camera equipment became a part of our traveling road show. He filmed the Phase I advocacy group as it did its community education work and the Phase II team as it did its campaign work.

The end result is the only documentary video to authentically capture the effort in real time. *Non-unanimous* premiered at the 2019 New Orleans Film Festival.[19] Donnellon has done cine-matography work for over thirty years. Looking back on the experi-ence, he is in awe of the magnitude of what he captured and extremely grateful that he acted on his concern instead of dismissing it or trusting that someone else would take up the mantle.

"At a time when the country is so deeply divided amongst partisan and racial lines, I managed to document a case of bipartisan, diverse collaboration and, through the documentary, was able to show the tremendous good that can come from efforts like this," says filmmaker Donnellon. Works like this can have both present and long-term impacts and that, according to him, explains part of why they are so important. Documentaries can teach lessons when a living teacher is not present or available and they can teach those lessons for many generations.

Donnellon feels cinematography is also important to social move-ments because of the unique way it allows the viewer to see and hear from people who are on the front lines. It can do what the media might be unwilling to do in that it broadens the range of permissible speakers on issues of import. He continues, "While it's certainly not a replacement for reading in-depth books or articles, it serves as an accessible entry point for a broad audience," Donnellon explains. "When the audience can watch real people, hear their voices, and take in the circumstances of the story, it can be inspiring and generate a call to action for the cause," says Donnellon.

Attorney Kenyatta Barthelemy entered the world of cinematography through a very different door, but has emerged from the same exit point as Donnellon. As a law student, Barthelemy made her video *Black Jurors: Missing in Action or Missing by Practice?* to complete a course requirement.[20] That video was so impactful, it became part of a popular symposium that showcased leading voices on jury diversity.[21] Those in attendance left with the video as a resource for use in future conversations about jury participation by people of color.

That video has had tremendous impact in reaching a largely over-looked audience—those in the 20-year-old to 30-year-old age group. This experience has caused Kenyatta to better understand some of the shortcomings of law and litigation and to appreciate the way additional advocacy techniques work to accelerate social change. She explains, "If a picture says a thousand words, a video says a million, and it whispers those words directly into the ear of the viewer." She opted for a video to teach about the issue of jury diversity as opposed to writing a paper or article because she saw it as most ideal way to have a conversation with her peers.

"My age group primarily receives information through social media platforms," she says. "It was the dissemination of George Floyd's murder footage on social media that sparked a global uprising that was heavily driven by the younger generation," she continued. The results have her convinced of the need to focus more of her efforts in this arena. She says the response has been amazing. People gained a new appreciation for jury duty. They now understand it is service and they no longer seek to avoid it.

There were several documentaries produced about the Angola 3 case towards the ends of teaching the public about the case and educating on the harms of solitary confinement. One has an after-life that is worth discussing. *Herman's House,* made by Angad Singh Bhalla, was shown on the Public Broadcasting Station. After, a section of the Point of View (POV) website was devoted to further study of solitary confinement. That site has a specific section with materials for educators and organisers to use. One is a community engagement and education discussion guide.[22] I served as one of the three expert reviewers.

The POV site describes the guide as "an invitation to dialogue" that is "based on a belief in the power of human connection, designed for people who want to use *Herman's House* to engage family, friends, classmates, colleagues and communities."[23] The site continues, "In contrast to initiatives that foster debates in which participants try to convince others that they are right, this documentary envisions conversations undertaken in a spirit of openness in which people try to understand one another and expand their thinking by sharing viewpoints and listening actively." [24] Movies only help if they are viewed widely and if they provoke dialogue and action. Sites like this aid in accomplishing all three on a much broader scale and with an air of legitimacy due to the expert affiliations.

Lyrics

In 2018, New Orleans rap artist Jerome "5th Ward Weebie" Cosey found a way to get people bouncing to the voting booth. The late artist remixed a song, creating high-energy lyrics that encouraged people to use their power by casting a vote to end non-unanimous juries. His song, *Let Me Find Out (VOTE!),* causes a listener to shake and roll in ungodly ways for a good cause.[25] After telling listeners "ya better vote," 5th Ward Weebie rhythmically commands them to "make them politicians ride for ya." With a bounce and a sassy neck roll, he warns listeners, "Let me find out you are not registered to vote."

"Let me find out you didn't vote so we lost it." As the listener rocks with pleasure, the message "we gotta go vote; stress Amendment 2" is felt and heard and voters are educated about constitutional doctrine in the most subtle of ways. The accompanying video ends with the artist and performers all displaying the raised, balled, right fist (associated with the sentiment "all power to the people.").[26] The video makes no effort to rebrand 5th Ward Weebie. He and his dancers are recognizable to his fan base, people often overlooked and underestimated in change movements. Change agents should not overlook this strategy.

Still Images, Sculptures & Exhibits

Still images, sculptures and exhibits speak to the soul in a universal language. That's how segregation became acceptable. The Jim Crow imagery programmed a nation. They convinced people of the inferiority of Blacks. Never underestimate the power of images and remember that positive images are not enough to move the struggle for civil and human rights forward. Change agents must also show the unpleasant realities of oppression and injustice. Exhibits can provide a venue for processing social issues. Still images and sculptures can introduce or interpret social challenges, shape people's perceptions of the past and aid them in imagining a better future.

Through all three, control of narratives can be claimed and, in doing so, harmful stereotypes can be disrupted. One of the ways the BPP successfully built local, national and international support was through the use of imagery. Emory Douglass, the former BPP Minister of Culture, is one of the best examples of this. He said his art was intended to show causes of oppression, encourage self-empowerment and provoke a new level of consciousness. The images Douglas created for the BPP released the emotions behind the Black struggle and communicated the terms of a human struggle. They met the eye like a blow from a fist. They stopped the viewer in their tracks.

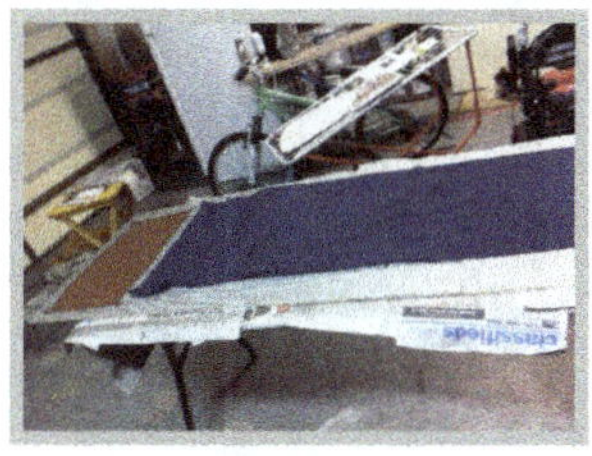

Photo credit Angela A. Allen-Bell.

In trying to teach about the harms of solitary confinement, my law students and I put these insights about imagery to work.

Photo credit Angela A. Allen-Bell. We did our artistic work with a minimal budget.

Photo credit Angela A. Allen-Bell.

When Congressman Dick Durbin (D-Il.) convened the first hearing on solitary confinement, a replica of a solitary confinement cell was on display.

Senate Judicial Subcommittee on the Constitution, Civil Rights and Human Rights, June 2012.

These examples demonstrate that the impact of a visual can be achieved with or without a budget and with or without formal training.

Senate Judicial Subcommittee on the Constitution, Civil Rights and Human Rights, June 2012.

These exhibits allowed people to experience the dimensions of solitary confinement and helped them appreciate the harms. It caused many emotional reactions and inspired future writing projects, legislative changes, scientific studies and advocacy efforts. Most importantly, they helped with empathy building. Each of the above examples serves as work under the truth-telling and memorialization pillars. As this is done, the groundwork is laid for future prosecutions, reparations and/or legal and policy reforms.

Using Media

According to Statista Research Department (SRD), in 2021 consumers around the world spent over 7.5 hours per day with media. SRD says Americans use media more than people in other parts of the world–around 347 minutes per day with traditional media, 470 minutes daily of digital media and radio consumption at least once a week. Media is amongst one of the most effective ways for advocates to communicate their messages. And it's not a new strategy for Blacks. Louisiana was home to *L'Union*,[27] the first Black newspaper in the South, and the *New Orleans Tribune*,[28] the first Black daily in the nation.

Both were created in the 1800's to elevate the concerns of Louisiana's Black population. These publications contained well-reasoned articles relative to citizenship, representation in government, voting rights, segregation and discrimination. They were respected publications with a broad readership, which included the Union army, state and federal legislators and more. Northern newspapers often reprinted their articles. They inspired local, national and international action and responses, including adoption of Louisiana's 1868 Constitution. Change agents should always assist with stories that are being written.

Assistance can be through the provision of documents, leads, contacts, information or quotes. It is a mistake to wait on that invitation. Until it comes or if it never comes, change agents should pen stories and op-eds to further understanding of the issue and to garner support. National newspapers, websites and magazines are great options, but newsletters, local print media, online sites, radio or television should be considered also. Interviews are also a good way of educating the public about issues. When doing them, talking points should be prepared in advance and they should list points by order of importance since time constraints will always be an issue.

You should also have a "call to action" prepared so the audience leaves with unequivocal instructions about what you would like done. After discussing the plight of the Angola 3 during a radio interview, I provided listeners with specific ways they could assist. Expressing opposition to the continued prosecution of the Angola 3 defendants was one of several calls to action that I provided that day. Listeners were given names and contact information for specific individuals associated with the prosecution. Later, an unknown listener shared a copy of this email:

Tue 6/9/2015 8:11 PM

To: XXXXXX

I find you to be an abhorrent human being. I have no doubt that your motivation to appeal the order by U.S. District Judge James Brady is some warped political move that I believe will ultimately fail. But due to the worst-ever miscarriage of justice in America being carried on for even seconds longer, much less days at your doing begs for you the label of an abhorrent human being. Your smiling face on the state website is disgusting. I cannot comprehend what Albert Woodfox has endured for decades at the hands of true criminals, state-sanctioned criminals, but to imagine that someone such as yourself can go to such an extent to continue to perpetrate the injustice AND CAN GET AWAY WITH IT! is beyond my mind's ability to grasp. I have many expletives I'm holding back but know not one of them is harsh enough to ever truly label you. I look forward to the day, either through retirement or otherwise that you are no longer able to harm others. And I really look forward to the day Albert walks free.

It's likely a coincidence, but that same year the recipient lost his bid for reelection.

If there is a group, a spokesperson must be selected. That person must be knowledgeable about the topic, effective as a communicator and disciplined in the face of public disagreement. Don't assume the most powerful or most senior person in your organization is the best spokesperson. Media collaborations can also be used towards the ends of fact-finding, truth-seeking or data collection (discussed further in "Use of Data, Science or Research").

Use of Other Written Communications

There is a range of written communications to consider beyond written legislative statements or print media stories. White papers, policy papers, newsletters, press releases, blogs, social media posts, email lists, listservs and scholarly publications are written communication tools that advocates should consider and be capable of using. Advocacy communications focus on influencing specific audiences and using specific messages in order to deliver changes in policy or practice.[29]

"In general, successful advocacy communications require clear objectives, knowledge of the intended audience, language appropriate for that audience and content that is short, specific and to the point."[30] "Ideally, these communications should be supported by an advocacy communications strategy which should include a section on how different pieces of communications will be monitored and evaluated. "[31] At all times, change agents must utilize the written word effectively and persuasively. Charts, graphs, images and embedded videos are particularly helpful so they should be considered during the drafting process.

As I did my non-unanimous jury community work, many people told me how easy the short videos that *The Advocate* included with its *Tilting the Scales Series* made it for them to quickly understand a complicated legal issue like non-unanimous juries.

Photo credit Lynda Woolard.

Lynda Woolard boasts of the tremendous role printed materials played in the success of the UJC. Lynda says the campaign used banners, yard signs, boards (shown above), t-shirts, water bottles, drawstring bags, fans, messages, buttons, door hangers, trifold brochures and pledge-to- vote cards (below). Woolard felt the quick message on such a broad range of mediums drove the point home to a broad range of people and in ways that generated the least resistance. She found the pledge to vote cards especially helpful in increasing voter turnout and database creation. "We were able to add supporters to our lists, and then send a postcard to voters in their own handwriting as a reminder to vote," says Woolard.

Photo credit Lynda Woolard.

Formal letters are another useful method of written communication. Change agents often underestimate the magnitude of what can be accomplished through formal letters. Advocates who write letters for social change use their own voices, which is empowering and likely more natural than the other advocacy approaches that are less innate. These letters allow advocates direct communication with the person having the power to effect change.

The Soldier's Medal for heroism, given for what Hugh Thompson did to protect unarmed civilians at My Lai, resulted from a series of letters Professor David Egan wrote. "Egan enlisted the support not only of former Presidential cabinet members, congressmen and senators, but also retired Army officers, military historians, veterans groups and finally print and electronic news media."[32] "With the assistance and encouragement of his wife, Jeannie, Egan would write more than a hundred letters to people in positions of influence, and most would respond favorably."[33]

The social turmoil that followed the murder of George Floyd prompted retired Chief Judge Bernette Johnson to author an open letter. In that letter, she expressed that the national protests of 2020 "are the consequence of centuries of institutionalized racism that has plagued our legal system." She continued, "Our prison population did not increase fivefold from 7,200 in 1978, to 40,000 in 2012 without decisive action over many years by the legislature and by prosecutors, juries and judges around the state.

We are part of the problem they protest." Her letter prompted action in the form of mandatory implicit bias training for all Louisiana judges elected in or after 2022.[34] Similarly, my efforts to end non-unanimous juries included a 2016 letter-writing campaign. My first mailing included over one hundred copies of this letter sent to members of the bar, legislature and criminal justice stakeholders:

September 13, 2016

Enclosed you will find an article I authored about Louisiana's non-unanimous jury system in non-capital, criminal cases....Beyond its racist origins, there are legitimate Sixth Amendment implications to maintaining such a law. Additionally, there are adverse policy considerations and the obvious fact that this law is a contributor to Louisiana's harrowing mass incarceration problem. With the laudable aim of restorative justice in mind, it is my opinion that the state of Louisiana must openly acknowledge this tainted part of its legal history and embrace change—the abolition of this practice. As stewards of the justice system, we are responsible for the quality of justice as much as we are tasked with seeking needed improvements to the legal system. Perhaps the solution will be brought about through our joined efforts. I would be honored if you would review my article. More importantly, I ask that you use your voice to generate meaningful action and dialogue around this very overdue conversation. Sincerely, Angela A. Allen-Bell

Tomiko Shine, Cultural Anthropologist and Founding Director of the Aging People in Prison Human Rights Campaign (APP-HRC), has taken letter-writing to new heights. For the past five years, she has organized group letter-writing campaigns where participants assemble to write letters supporting the release of aging women and men who have been incarcerated for many decades. Because many volunteers lack familiarity with the specific cases, generational incarceration or the carceral state, preliminary education sessions are completed before the letters are composed.

The letters produced during these "Freedom Campaigns" are sent to parole boards, governors, judges or lawyers. Shine describes APP-HRC's work as "an attempt to achieve reparations in the form of bodies." As a secondary goal, APP-HRC seeks policy changes that amplify human rights protections. Shine says the best evidence of the usefulness of these group letter-writing campaigns is the fact that the pressure of a multitude of voices has led to the release of several aging men and women who might not have seen freedom were it not for the evidence of community support.

Shine cites additional benefits, such as the way these group letter-writing campaigns: call attention to the plight of aging prisoners; alert state officials that they are being watched and opposed; inculcate youth and young activists into social movements; inspire hope in the justice-impacted who often have lost family members and support and exist in a state of despair; and, the potential to transform the imprudent conversations about mass incarceration to one about human rights.

When engaging in community education work, change agents must disavow the notion that those paid to perform a job will do so. Advocates should approach their work with the understanding that the duty to teach and change is theirs and not always the person whose job description says they should be doing this work. As you teach and attempt change, people in the audience will be prompted to act in various ways. Some will be jurors on cases. Others will show up for hearings or court dates. Others will write, speak or otherwise educate about the cause. Many will be voters. These sessions with the public can transform your cause and make it a movement. As you view these next images, consider the different audiences and the way they are uniquely qualified to act once educated about a cause.

Margarie Esman, Angela A. Allen-Bell & Will Snowden. Photo credit Brooke Bell.

As a panel, we spoke to law students, lawyers and community members about the harms of non-unanimous juries at the 2017 National Lawyers Guild gathering at Loyola Law School in New Orleans.

Photo credit Justin Bullard.

Here, at the invitation of the SULC Black Law Students Association, I am training law students to speak about the harms of using non-unanimous juries in Louisiana.

Photo credit Calvin Duncan.

At the invitation of the NAACP and the St. Tammany Indivisible Chapter, I shared my research on non-unanimous juries at an Abita Springs, Louisiana gathering.

Photo credit Tracie Taylor.

On this evening, at the invitation of the late Professor Rebecca Hensley and the Justice4All student organisation, I spoke to college students at Southeastern Louisiana University about the importance of ending non-unanimous juries.

Drama Club
Presenting
Rev. E. Phares Vicint, Sr.
Non-Unanimous Jury Law Presentation (10/2)

"Featuring"
Southern University Law Center
Professor, Angela A. Allen-Bell

A-Building
5:30pm - 8:30pm

To attend please sign up before May 21, 2018

At the invitation of the Angola Drama Club, I spoke to men convicted by non-unanimous juries about the advocacy effort.

N.O. Bar Association 12/20/16 CLE Emily Maw, Allen-Bell & Ed Tarpley. Photo credit Marjorie Esman.

I joined Emily Maw and Ed Tartly in a presentation about non-unanimous juries for lawyers who attended a continuing legal education event sponsored by the New Orleans Bar Association.

Photo credit Ben Donnellon.

Robin Schulberg organised a presentation for the St. Tammany Parish Democratic Party Precinct Organizing Committee so they could understand the issue before they started their door-to-door canvasing efforts.

Photo Credit Sherri Rhodes.

I spoke at a community voting rally. In the audience were community members, students, academics and public officials.

Angela A. Allen-Bell and her cousin. Photo Credit Sherri Rhodes.

Below, I'm speaking to high school students about the kind of legal issues lawyers must confront. I used a box to construct a space that is the equivalent of a solitary confinement cell, which is the functional equivalent of a parking spot. As I speak, I allow audience members to enter upon the condition that they will imagine walls and life there with no human contact.

Photo credit to Briana Bell.

When doing the work of community education, change agents must remember that voters, jurors, influencers, law and policy makers and justice officials are seated in these audiences. Change agents should never underestimate any audience member. Case in point—none of the men in the Angola audience could vote, but all of them understood the harm to follow a conviction by a non-unanimous jury. They were unrecognized experts. Acting upon fears for their children and loved ones, these experts urged family and friends to vote.

Many of their affiliates weren't registered voters. A plea from them led people to participate in a way that few others could have. Change agents should notice how these audiences are diverse in age, geography, education, politics, power and race (as the deliberative process research encourages). Efforts fail where exclusion is practiced. After many of these talks, audience members shared how they took the information they learned to their social and professional circles, which means a single message was disseminated to an incalculable number of people. Change agents must also know how these examples serve the aims of the truth-telling and memorialization pillars. As this is done, the groundwork is laid for future prosecutions, reparations and/or legal and policy reforms.

<u>Using the Past to Inform the Future</u>

Past events are rarely in the past. Change agents should seize opportunities to make these historical connections. Here are a few reasons why:

<u>Louis A. Martinet</u>

At the request of the Martinet family, I joined some of my students in a search for the tomb of Louis A. Martinet. Martinet was a medical doctor and a Louisiana activist-lawyer who, in the late 1800s, led the *Plessy v. Ferguson* strategy and founded The *Crusader* newspaper to fight racial injustice and segregation. When Martinet died in 1917 in New Orleans during the Jim Crow era, it appears his family was unable to host a public funeral. He was placed in a tomb, but his name was not added to the tomb. Over time, the location of his burial was forgotten. Law students Beau Ackal and Christopher Adkins located his tomb in 2023 and notified the Martinet family.

Photo credit Brian Martinet.

Family members purchased an appropriate marker for his tomb. On October 22, 2023, the family hosted a memorial service at Metairie Cemetery in New Orleans to honor his memory and to dedicate his marker. Efforts like this create a proper narrative about Black men. It showcases them as law-abiding, social engineers. This goes a long way toward countering biases and aids in efforts to void racial narratives and hierarchies. Both are needed for immediate legal system and long-term transformation. Consider how the understanding that this work brings can directly impact legislators, jurors, judges, prosecutors, law enforcement officers and probation officers as they perform their functions within the carceral state. Beyond this, work of this nature creates opportunities for monuments of celebrated legal players of color that can be erected as independent statements or as replacements for offensive monuments that must be removed.

Students United

Students United was a student-led campus movement for change at S.U. in Baton Rouge, the main campus in a university system that had the largest number of Black students in the country at the time. In an early 1970's publication of the People's College Press, Students United declared education was of no value if it did not "speak to the conditions of the oppressed" and did not "ensure . . . the upkeep of the nation." According to the group, S.U. was molding "minds that would submit to the tyranny that exploits and dehumanizes the people of the world" and preparing "a reservoir of lackeys to exploit Black and poor people worldwide." It wanted to transform S.U. so that the university would "aid in the building of a more humane society."

Beyond this goal, the students complained of inept administrators, a gross disparity in the way S.U. and other public institutions were funded, the absence of a legitimate grievance process, dilapidated buildings, rodent problems, poor healthcare provisions, substandard food, the need for department councils, a lack of curriculum content that was relevant to Black social consciousness, a disparity in the treatment of qualified instructors of color and white professors who were either inappropriate with students or ineffective, and a lack of attention to the needs of the neighboring Scotlandville Community. Students United called for the formation of a board of representatives that included faculty and students who could review and address student concerns about student life, policy, hiring, retention, and curricula and vote on important matters.

Though an HBCU, S.U. was operated by an all-white board of trustees and then-President George Leon Netterville was answerable to them. Students United presented their grievances to Netterville. When ignored, Students United penned numerous statements and letters and relentlessly attempted meetings and negotiations. Avoidance and inaction gave way to weeks of boycotts, demonstrations, and protests and then a demand for a change in leadership. Students United escalated their concerns to the now-defunct State Board of Education and even Governor Edwin Edwards. Demonstrations, boycotts and daily meetings continued on campus and even at the state capitol. Student participation was often in the ninetieth percentile. Officials responded with arrests.

On November 9, 1972, Students United members Ricky Hill and Nathaniel Howard were arrested and charged with obstruction or interference of educational processes and facilities. Organizing continued and more arrests followed. On November 16, 1972, Students United members Charlene "Sukari" Hardnett, Paul Shrivers, Fred Prejean, and Louis Anthony were arrested. Prejean was charged with criminal trespass, while the others were booked on obstruction or interference with an educational institution. These arrests prompted some students to visit Netterville's office on November 16, 1972, to plea for his assistance in securing the release of those in custody. After the meeting, he exited the building under the guise of assisting. Shortly thereafter, a call from S.U. was placed to law enforcement, falsely reporting that Netterville was being held hostage. Law enforcement officials descended upon the campus with weapons, artillery and a massive show of force.

Within moments two unarmed S.U. students—Denver Smith and Leonard Brown—were dead at the hands of law enforcement. Students Leonard Jackson and James E. Jackson were also wounded. While no university, state, or law enforcement official has ever been held accountable in civil or criminal court, the FBI and several local commissions and bodies issued findings in the aftermath. As the campus community mourned, some members of Students United were in court fighting civil injunctions jointly initiated by S.U. and the State Board of Education. Dubbed ringleaders by state and university officials, the following Students United members were "restrained, enjoined and prohibited from entering on the campus": Charlene Hardnett, Ricky Hill, Nathaniel Howard, Herget Harris, Paul Shivers, Louis J. Anthony, Donald Mills, Willie T. Henderson and Fred Prejean. Because of these civil and/or criminal cases, most of them had to abandon their studies or pursue their education elsewhere.

Following its investigation, a State Attorney General's Committee of Inquiry found that S.U. "had not developed a well-prepared plan to ensure that students could provide responsible contributions to the conduct of university life." It also found that "no university personnel were held hostage or forcibly detained," and it determined that the report of a hostage situation caused the nonviolent students to be met with inhumane force by law enforcement officers. The investigation also found that the "number and variety of weapons brought on campus by law enforcement . . . was far more than necessary to deal with an unarmed group of students."

Photo credit: Angela A. Allen-Bell

However, the investigation did not completely exonerate the students. It concluded that Students United exceeded the "bounds of constitutionally guaranteed protest and created disorder on the campus." A separate inquest by the Black People's Committee of Inquiry, led by Black elected officials and leaders, felt otherwise. It determined that the students acted in good faith and S.U. officials acted in bad faith and "effected a flagrantly political use of the judicial process to suppress legitimate student dissent." On November 16, 2022, for the fiftieth anniversary of the campus tragedy, my students and I hosted a narrative change and racial healing program where student leaders from 1972 could, for the first time since the murders in 1972, assemble to speak their truth about their organizing and the events that led up to that day.

Photo credit Brittany Dunn.

My requests for official action were generously granted. That night, Students United received a proclamation from the Office of Mayor-

President Sharon Weston Broome and a commendation from the Louisiana Legislative Black Caucus. Governor John Bel Edwards issued his second *Amende Honorable,* a historical form of formal reparation for an offense done by making an open and humbling acknowledgment and apology to restore the victim's honor, to the Smith and Brown families, to Students United and to the S.U. Community. For the first time in over fifty years, a counternarrative had been created.

It established these, now senior citizens, to be intellectuals who led a credible, non-violent movement. More importantly, it showed how law was used to harm. It established them as victims. It presented an opportunity for the state to take a degree of accountability. In doing so, respect for the rule of law was renewed and lawlessness on the part of governmental actors was officially disavowed. These actions set a standard for transition (if there is a collective commitment to transition to follow). This work under the prevention of reoccurrence, truth-seeking and memorialization pillars can help inform reparations, which help build confidence in the transition. It also helps to achieve future legal and policy reforms, as well as inspire a vision for the kinds of things that the transitioned legal system should and should not do.

"Cuttin' Cane A'int All We Do" Exhibit

In 2019, the West Baton Rouge Parish Museum curated the *"Cuttin' Cane A'int All We Do"* Exhibit, which explored a range of themes from the slavery era to the civil rights era. Kathe Hambrick, then Curator and Director of Interpretation at the WBRM, described the exhibit as a "story of survival that includes videos about the people of Louisiana and the laws that governed them after emancipation." Dr. Angelique Bergeron, Executive Director of the WBRM, indicated that the exhibit was offered "because we feel it is crucial to tell a more complete story of the people who shaped our communities. We hope these videos help to frame our history, in both the struggles and accomplishments, and leave viewers with a sense of pride and a call to action."

I contributed content to videos that Bergeron references.[35] They played in the slave cabins within the exhibit. A middle and high school curriculum accompanied the exhibit. This truth-seeking work helps society reckon with its past and reconstruct its future. It helps us assess and understand the sources of systemic failures so, during transition, they can be addressed and eradicated. It helps promote anti-racism principles and it offers compelling reasons for abandoning the human hierarchy. Insofar as reforms to the legal system, this type of memorialization work can make it possible for people who doubt system failure is possible to see through documented examples that it is. It can also create the will to reimagine systems that fail and to begin the work of transitioning them.

Colfax Massacre

During the 1872 election for Louisiana's next governor, the ballot was evenly split between Democratic and Republican candidates. This led to the formation of supremacy groups such as the White League, a domestic terrorist group that employed tactics similar to the Ku Klux Klan. Sentiments erupted on April 13, 1873, when the fear of Republicans seizing control over the Grant Parish government in Colfax, Louisiana, caused a mob of more than 150 armed white men to surround the courthouse. Once the courthouse was surrounded, and while several defenders fought from a shallow trench, a cannon was fired on the men inside. When defenders retreated into the courthouse, the roof was set on fire.

Despite an attempt to surrender, the indiscriminate killing of Blacks continued well into the night. In the end, mass numbers of Black men were murdered and at least three white men were killed. The killing and destruction did not stop there. White supremacists continued their reign of terror and unrelentingly killed random Blacks in-not only Grant-but also in surrounding parishes. Federal prosecutors used federal legislation to bring the white vigilantes to justice. In *United States v. Cruikshank*, the SCOTUS reversed the convictions of the white vigilantes, reasoning that the federal government had exceeded its authority in getting involved with what the SCOTUS deemed a state matter. This decision blocked federal efforts to prosecute hate crimes against Blacks. In so doing, it gave sanction to further acts of domestic terrorism upon the newly emancipated people as they innocently attempted to experience the citizenship that had recently been bestowed on them.

The ruling triggered an end to Reconstruction in the South and opened the door for white supremacists to have their way without fear of repercussions. In 1951, a monument at the site of the Colfax Massacre was erected. It described the massacre as the "riot that marked the end of carpetbag misrule in the South" and it commemorated the three white men who lost their lives. Because the marker offensively and inaccurately depicted the slaughter of innocent Black men asserting their constitutional rights, two descendants joined forces to do the overdue and necessary work of narrative change. Reverend Avery Hamilton worked for years to have the marker removed. He, along with several other concerned citizens, petitioned the Grant Parish Police Jury to take it down, to no avail. It was not until after Dean Woods sent a letter to the Assistant Secretary of the Louisiana Economic Department did things begin to change.

Those officials met with the Police Jury and convinced them that the state of Louisiana owned the marker and wanted it taken down. The Police Jury relented. The marker was finally removed on May 15, 2021. Reverend Avery Hamilton is the great-great-great grandson of formerly enslaved Jesse McKinney, the first casualty of the Colfax Massacre who was murdered in his front yard a few days prior. Dean Woods is a retired businessman who resides in

Houston, Texas. Dean was grief-stricken by the revelation that his great-grandfather was one of the men who participated in the massacre.

Reverend Avery Hamilton and Dean Woods. Photo credit David Bell.

Since then, Dean has committed himself to doing all that he can to make amends for his ancestor's actions. The two formed The Colfax Memorial Organization, a non-profit devoted to the work of correcting the false narratives surrounding one of the worst episodes of racial carnage of the Reconstruction era–the Colfax Massacre.

Rather than simply replace the historical marker with one containing the correct story, Avery and Dean felt more was needed.

These two unexpected friends desired to create a new monument and an accompanying reflective space that would properly honor and commemorate those who died fighting for their right to experience full citizenship through the exercise of the vote and democratic participation. My students and I assisted with their efforts to raise funds for the new monument. Through their incredible efforts and the help of so many (acting in the spirit of that deliberative process research discussed in *Diversity in the Jury Box*), that new monument was unveiled. For the first time, the world got a glimpse at the names of the Black massacre victims.

Photo credit David Bell.

This effort fulfils the aims of reparations insofar as it seeks to repair. It also serves the goals of truth-seeking and memorialization. Additionally, it allows victims to witness a government acknowledge its failure to protect all citizens. This helps create trust where it was once lacking and it allows for reconciliation. It gives an identity to the anonymous Blacks who were slaughtered. In doing so, it allows for empathy and creates the capacity for the world to view Black men as occasional victims. It disrupts the false narrative that Blacks are more violent than anyone else and showcases white people as a group capable of violence. This is not done for the purpose of denigrating the character of whites. It is done for the purpose of showcasing them as other than the standard of excellence by which all others are to be measured.

It shows them as a group with a range of assets and failures like all other groups. It equalizes people and destroys the hierarchy that ranks one group superior to all others. It inspires questions about other cases of domestic terrorism that whites may be responsible for. It forces dialogue over the lack of accountability that exists. It creates a framework to juxtapose the way Blacks, at the same time these countless massacres and lynchings happened, were held to the fullest extent of the law. It creates a clear picture of why the complexion of today's carceral state is not just or accurate. It compels sound reforms to laws, policies, practices and customs during transition.

Using Law & Policy to Achieve Justice and/or Change Policy

Change agents must be able to successfully navigate the landscape of both policy and law change. While the terms do share commonalities, there are important differences to recognize. Laws are rules that regulate the actions of people in a jurisdiction. Laws can be enforced by the imposition of penalties and must be followed by everyone in a jurisdiction. Private citizens cannot make laws. Laws can only be made by the legislative branch.

Policy, on the other hand, is the conscience of the citizens that is applied to matters of public health, safety, and welfare. It's the goals and objectives that a group establishes–the very things it seeks to achieve or seeks to avoid. It's a plan of action. One of the main purposes of government is to establish policy and have government workers carry it out. Unlike law, citizens can't face consequences for violating policy.

The beliefs and attitudes that shape policy are often the inspiration for laws. Conversely, law can cause policy creation in an effort to carry the law out. Consider these examples. A couple starting a family decide that, when their parenting years are over, they want to look back and conclude that they raised children with morals and principles. To achieve this, they prepare family rules that they will live by, such as weekly church attendance, required book readings, community service and family interaction nights at regular intervals. They impose consequences when rules are broken.

The goal of raising children with morals and values can be considered the policy. The rules can be considered the law. In the second example, speeders kill ducks that regularly cross city streets. As a policy intended to address speeding, the jurisdiction installs speed bumps and duck crossing signs. As a law, the crime of speeding is created and consequences are imposed upon violators.

Change agents must become acquainted with policy because of the way it translates into priority for a jurisdiction, because of the way it inspires laws and influences sentencing and because of its potential for being a more expeditious pathway to changes than law. As an initial measure, change agents must be able to identify existing policies. The most ideal way of doing so is through express statements that are codified in law, such as in the instance of La. R.S. 36:2 (C), which states:

> *It is the public policy of this state*...to create a structure for the executive branch...which is responsive to the needs of the people... which is sufficiently flexible to meet changing human and natural conditions; to promote economy and efficiency...and to strengthen the executive capacity for effective, efficient, and economic administration at all levels; to improve the quality of the functions

performed and the programs and services rendered...to conserve and enhance...natural resources of the state; to provide that the responsibility of the respective departments for the implementation of programs and policies is clearly fixed and ascertainable; and to eliminate...duplication of effort...to use wisely the funds of the state....

Attorney Will Harrell, a graduate of American University Washington College of Law (JD and LL.M. in International Human Rights), has extensive experience doing policy work in Louisiana and the Gulf South. He is Senior Public Policy Counsel at VOTE and also the founder and director of the Justice Collaborative, LLC, a criminal and juvenile justice consulting firm. According to attorney Harrell, "change agents should know that there is no single way of identifying existing policy." Beyond finding it incorporated in legislation, Attorney Harrell says policy might be cited in agency press releases or communications, such as this:

January 2022

**U.S. Commission on Civil Rights Policy Statement
on Sexual Orientation and Gender Identity
Discrimination**

It is the policy of the U.S. Commission on Civil Rights to provide a workplace free from discrimination on the basis of sexual orientation or gender identity….Executive Order 13,087…further provides:

> It is the policy of the government of the United States to provide equal opportunity in federal employment for all persons, to prohibit discrimination in employment because of race, color, religion, sex, national origin, handicap, age, sexual orientation or status as a parent, and to promote the full realization of equal employment opportunity through a continuing affirmative program in each executive department and agency. This policy of equal opportunity applies to and must be an integral part of every aspect of personnel policy and practice in the employment, development, advancement, and treatment of civilian employees of the federal government, to the extent permitted by law.

Harrell says "existing policy can also be found in the administrative rules that set forth regulations, processes and procedures for government agencies, through executive orders, through the implementation of laws or by observing public and private meetings of boards, commissions and/or organizations or even through the award of reparations."[36] Policy can even be communicated by the President during the State of the Union address or by the act of vetoing legislative acts.

Much of Attorney Harrell's work involves creating policies when they are lacking or changing existing policies. In reflecting on his over thirty years of policy work, he says change agents must possess four attributes if they wish to achieve success in this area. Attorney

Harrell describes them as: "(1) power mapping (identifying who has the power to make changes and strategizing on how best to get that person to act in the desired way); (2) knowing the rules, procedures and powers of the agencies and bodies that you approach; (3) knowing how to form and foster relationships with opponents and people in positions of power; and, (4) engaging in respectful interactions with others (both supporters and opponents)."

Attorney Harrell advises change agents seeking to change existing policy or establish new policy to first approach the agency or body cloaked with the authority to do what is wanted. "Through these conversations where both parties explain their positions, compromises can result and agreements can be reached," Harrell notes. If that fails, he says, "you don't wave the surrender flag." You must become more imaginative. He mentioned tricks that he pulls out his hat at times like this. One is working with private industry or academics to establish best practices or with the executive branch to secure executive orders that can serve to leverage future conversations that might not have yielded the desired results the first time. Attorney Harrell tells that the path to policy creation is not always a linear one:

> When I set out to establish or change policy and end up with a resolution agreeing to study an issue, I now have the wisdom to see the great potential in this outcome. When people are assigned to study an issue in this way, an immediate venue for conversation is created. Relationships are developed. Fears and concerns are revealed through conversations. Trust is developed.

"Change agents should embrace these detours instead of becoming frustrated by them," says Harrell. He also explains that policy work is not for the impatient. Attorney Harrell warns, in the world of policy work, there is never a right time to declare a victory. "Policy must be implemented by humans. Sometimes they are resistant so they ignore adopted policy, which means what seemed like a success can prove to be a failure in the end," says Harrell. He's lived this a few times.

He served as a federal monitor for the juvenile justice system in Ohio and as an independent Ombudsman retained to monitor juvenile justice changes in Texas. "In both instances," explains Harrell, "there were clear policy directives to follow. But not everyone wanted to conform to those policies. I was there to monitor and guide implementation." Because of this, Harrell says "change agents should understand the perpetual nature of policy work—at any given time, they will be creating, changing or monitoring compliance with or impact of policy."

Many of the forthcoming strategies are useful towards the achievement of policy change so they should be considered as a complement to the insights shared in this section. However, Harrell insists that none of them will serve you better than "relationship capital." It is wise to remember that, "in the south, culture will eat strategy for breakfast."[37] Whether it's law or policy change, scholar and historian Ibram X. Kendi urges greater attention to the outcome and less attention to the intention behind law or policy.[38]

<u>Law</u>

Law reforms can be accomplished in a few ways. Sometimes litigation prompts the legislature to act. Other times, the public—through individual requests or group demands—become the inspiration for laws. As previously explained, when one does the work of law change in Louisiana, they are actually fulfilling a prophecy. Louisiana defines legislation as the "solemn expression of legislative will." By design, that "will" should reflect the pulse of the people. The process fails if people don't involve themselves in the legislative process. With the advent of social media, that has become nearly effortless. Every member of Congress has a Twitter account and most local officials do, as well. Many members of legislative bodies also use other social media options for public engagement. The next section speaks to those wishing to engage in person (in Louisiana, in another state or with Congress).

<u>Inside the Legislature</u>

The Louisiana legislature is composed of two chambers: the House of Representatives and the Senate. Individual legislators are assigned to committees. Each committee has limited jurisdiction over certain matters. Change agents must identify the committee(s) that have jurisdiction over their area of interest. At intervals, the Louisiana legislature convenes for legislative sessions, a block of time within which the legislature meets for the purpose of lawmaking. In Louisiana, there are five types of legislative sessions: organizational, emergency, extraordinary (special), regular, and veto. The lawmaking process begins with a bill.

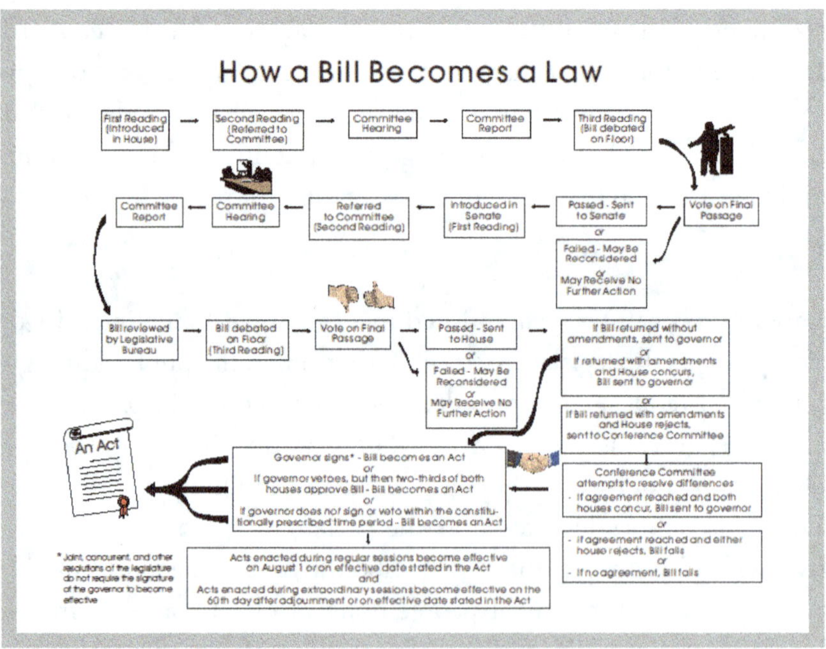

Louisiana State Legislature (found at <u>Louisiana State Legislature</u>)

Bills are the starting point for proposed laws. Bills are often modified as they are discussed and debated at the legislative committee stage. These committees exist in both the House and Senate. At this stage in the process, stakeholders and the general public can present verbal or written testimony (or both) to the committee in an effort to influence their vote. These hearings are public proceedings.

The schedules are available on the website of the Louisiana State Legislature. There are a variety of ways for citizens to participate in the lawmaking process. One is through speaking to delegations within the legislature. For example, during the non-unanimous jury campaign, I spoke to members of the Legislative Black Caucus and shared my research and opinion as to why Louisiana should end its use of non-unanimous juries.

Angela A. Allen-Bell after a presentation to lawmakers. Photo credit Rep. Edmond Jordan

A second way of participating in the law-making process is by submitting concerns to the committee in writing. Any person who does not feel comfortable giving testimony in person may submit a prepared statement in accordance with House Rule 14.33 in lieu of appearing before the committee.[39] If this is done, clearly state your position and succinctly offer support as illustrated in the following example:

September 5, 2024

Honorable Chair John C. "Jay" Morris III
Senate Committee on Judiciary C
Louisiana State Senate
P.O. Box 94183
Baton Rouge, Louisiana 70804

RE: Hearing on D.A. Jason Williams' Use/Grant
of Post Conviction Relief

Dear Chair Morris and Members of Senate Committee on Judiciary C:

I am a law professor and have been for over twenty years. I teach Criminal Procedure and Constitutional Law and both are areas of scholarly interest. From this perspective, I humbly offer some insights on today's hearing involving the New Orleans District Attorney's Office's use of post conviction relief. I ask that this communication be made part of the official record of this proceeding.

District Attorney Jason Williams has properly exercised the powers of his office. The Louisiana State Constitution intentionally grants broad powers to district attorneys. On a prior occasion when an individual accused a district attorney of misconduct and attempted to interrupt a district attorney's use of the powers of his office, the Louisiana's Supreme Court registered the following objection:

Article V, § 26 of the Louisiana Constitution of 1974 provides the district attorney with broad and sweeping powers as part and parcel of his role as the state's prosecuting attorney. A district attorney is a constitutional officer who serves in the judicial branch and exercises a portion of the sovereign power of the state within the district of his office. *The district attorney has entire charge and control of every criminal prosecution instituted or pending in his district and determines whom, when and how he shall prosecute.* Furthermore, there is no provision of law that defines or limits the type of cases a district attorney may prosecute. Finally, the jurisdiction of the district attorney to prosecute those who violate state criminal statutes is exclusive; it can only be constrained or curtailed when it operates to the prejudice of a contrary constitutional mandate, and even then only with *due deference to the district attorney's constitutional prerogative.*

For fear of this being dismissed as a lone incident, I offer yet another instance of the Louisiana Supreme Court confronting the very issue this committee is convened over today. In this second instance, a citizen also attempted to stop a district attorney from performing his statutory duties. Yet again, the Louisiana Supreme Court observed the impropriety of this. Significantly, the court observed that "*it is as much the duty of the district attorney to see that no innocent man suffers as it is to see that no guilty man escapes.*" That same opinion references the views of the SCOTUS on the matter. According to the SCOTUS, "a prosecutor is the representative not of an ordinary party to a controversy, but of a sovereignty *whose obligation to govern impartially is as compelling as its obligation to govern at all; and whose interest, therefore, in a criminal prosecution is not that it shall win a case, but that justice shall be done. As such, he is... the servant of the law.*" It is worth noting that the Louisiana District Attorneys Association filed an amicus curiae brief in this case where they also echoed the very sentiments that I express today.

District Attorney Jason Williams fully complied with Louisiana's post conviction laws. The legislature wrote the post conviction laws that D.A. Jason Williams used in such a way that the D.A. has discretion. In each instance, he acted within the bounds of that discretion. Beyond that, article 930.10 in the Code of Criminal Procedure allows the D.A. to "deviate from any of the provisions" of Louisiana's post convictions laws.

There are adverse implications to be considered by this body. If this one D.A. must answer to the legislature for the way discretion was used on select cases, shouldn't all D.A.'s do the same since they all make discretionary calls about who to take to trial, when to offer a plea, whether to seek appellate review, etc. If the legislature meets with each elected official to oversee each discretionary call they make, are the wishes of voters undermined when the person they elected to make decisions is prevented from doing so? Does this effort constitute government entanglement? Are there racial implications to questioning a Black man's intellectual capacity to make a decision? Does this give the appearance of bias since no white prosecutor has been called before this body about their discretionary decisions (in a state where the governor just issued an executive order expressing disdain for divisive concepts)? Does this effort undermine checks and balances? Since this effort is motivated by public safety concerns, should this committee extend its inquiry to the excessively high rate of wrongful convictions in the state and to the epidemic proportions of prosecutorial misconduct that the SCOTUS has repeatedly observed in Louisiana?

I have studied the post conviction actions in question and the D.A.'s Civil Rights Unit in general. I stand firm in my conclusions that the post conviction decisions were properly vetted and that the unit is a model that should be replicated throughout the state. I am willing to dialogue further. I am also willing to work in conjunction with this committee to achieve justice improvements in the state so please consider me a resource. Thanks in advance for your attention to my concerns. As a crime victim, I especially thank you for your efforts to ensure public safety.

Sincerely,

Angela A. Allen-Bell

B.K. Agnihotri Endowed Professor

If you have a legislative proposal in mind or a solution that you would like the committee to consider, it is appropriate to present them in your written communication. When I did this in response to a federal legislative hearing on solitary confinement, beyond the statements being maintained in the official government records, these statements were housed on "Solitary Watch's" website.

06.19.12

Durbin Chairs First-Ever Congressional Hearing On Solitary Confinement

[WASHINGTON, D.C.] – Assistant Majority Leader Dick Durbin (D-IL) chaired a hearing today on the issue of solitary confinement in the nation's prisons, jails and detention centers. The hearing, held before the Senate Judiciary Committee's Subcommittee on the Constitution, Civil Rights and Human Rights, focused on the human rights, fiscal and public safety consequences of solitary confinement.

"The United States holds more prisoners in solitary confinement than any other democratic nation in the world," Durbin said. "The dramatic expansion of the use of solitary confinement is a human rights issue we can't ignore. We can no longer slam the cell door and turn our backs on the impact our policies have on the mental state of the incarcerated and ultimately on the safety of our nation."

During the last several decades, the United States has witnessed an explosion in the use of solitary confinement for federal, state, and local prisoners and detainees. Today, more than 2.3 million people are imprisoned in the United States. This is – by far – the highest per capita rate of incarceration in the world.

Solitary confinement - also called supermax housing, segregation and isolation – is designed to separate inmates from each other and isolate them for a variety of reasons. Originally used to segregate the most violent prisoners in the nation's supermax prisons, the practice is increasingly being used and for vulnerable groups like immigrants, children and LGBT inmates – supposedly for their own protection. According to the Bureau of Justice Statistics, the United States held over 80,000 people in some kind of restricted detention. In Illinois, 56% of inmates have spent some time in segregated housing.

Prisoners in isolation are often confined to small cells without windows, with little to no access to the outside world. Inmates are confined to these cells for up to 23 hours a day. Such extreme isolation can have serious psychological effects on inmates and – as Craig Haney, Professor of Psychology at the University of California, Santa Cruz testified to the Subcommittee – can lead to mental illness, self-mutilation and a "disturbingly high" rate of suicide. According to several state and national studies, at least half of all prison suicides occur in solitary confinement. Photographs of a typical solitary cell can be found here.

In addition to the impact solitary confinement has on inmates, there are also public safety and fiscal concerns with the practice. The bipartisan Commission on Safety and Abuse in America's Prisons found that the use of solitary confinement often increased acts of violence in prions. Further, it is extremely costly to house a prisoner in solitary confinement. In Tamms, Illinois' only supermax prison, it costs more than $60,000 a year to house a prisoner in solitary confinement compared to an average of $22,000 for inmates in other prisons.

"All of these issues lead to the obvious conclusion: we need to reassess solitary confinement and honestly reform policies which do not make us safer," Durbin said.

A panel of experts, including a former exonerated inmate who spent 18 years incarcerated and in solitary confinement, testified at today's hearing. The witnesses were: Charles Samuels, Director, Federal Bureau of Prisons; Stuart M. Andrews Jr., Partner, Nelson Mullins Riley & Scarborough LLP; Christopher Epps, Commissioner of the Mississippi Department of Corrections; Anthony Graves, Founder, Anthony Believes; and Dr. Craig Haney, Professor of Psychology, University of California, Santa Cruz. Copies of their testimony and Senator Durbin's opening remarks are attached.

Video of today's hearing can be found at www.judiciary.senate.gov. This was the second hearing Senator Durbin has chaired focusing on human rights issues in US prisons. The first looked at the treatment of mentally ill inmates in US prisons. More information about that hearing can be found here.

Amongst them were statements from people impacted by solitary confinement, medical experts, corrections officials, academics and many others. These statements became a quick resource for stakeholders, policy makers and other interested parties. They continue to be used for organizing, legislating, researching and advocating around this issue.

Reassessing Solitary Confinement: The Human Rights, Fiscal,
and Public Safety Consequences

Hearing Before the Senate Judiciary Subcommittee on the Constitution,
Civil Rights, and Human Rights

The Honorable Dick Durbin, Chair

Tuesday, June 19, 2012
Written Statement Submitted by:
Professor Angela A. Allen-Bell
Southern University Law Center
P.O. Box 9294
Baton Rouge, Louisiana 70813-9294

I begin with an expression of immense gratitude to Senator Dick Durbin and the Senate Subcommittee on the Constitution, Civil Rights, and Human Rights for having the compassion, courage and fortitude to explore an issue that promises no personal advancement for anyone. Efforts relative to the issue of solitary confinement and its abuses are patently selfless and profoundly pious. Work on behalf of vulnerable and disesteemed inmates yields few monetary rewards and invites a barrage of cynicism. Thank you for exemplifying leadership and for undertaking this long overdue expedition and for spearheading this much needed inquest.

I recently authored an article where I examined some of the constitutional issues surrounding solitary confinement practices in the United States. The article is published in the spring 2012 issue of the Hastings Constitutional Law Quarterly. The article is titled: *"Perception Profiling & Prolonged Solitary Confinement Viewed Through The Lens of The Angola 3 Case: When Prison Officials Become Judges, Judges Become Visually Challenged and Justice Becomes Legally Blind."* While the article uses the case of the Angola 3, two Louisiana men who have been held in solitary confinement for **40 years**, as a case study, the article should in no way be viewed as a work that is limited in nature to the case of the Angola 3. Instead, the article uses cases and authorities from across the nation in an attempt to study the issue of prolonged solitary confinement. What was revealed in the end was the fact that the Angola 3's case was in no way an isolated incident or a paranormal event. The fate of the Angola 3 is representative of a documented, dangerous trend in penal institutions whereby many inmates are subject to solitary confinement despite having committed absolutely no infraction behind prison walls and, once there, are trapped for indefinite or permanent periods because there is no meaningful review process in place and because there is a lack of judicial oversight.

My article discusses three constitutional concerns relative to current prolonged isolation practices, the first of which is due process. The article discusses how a meaningful process can and should be afforded to inmates when their stay in prolonged isolation is evaluated at periodic intervals. Thereafter, the article addresses how the current prolonged isolation practices undermine the Doctrine of Separation of Powers. This is followed by an explanation of how and why judicial abstention has led to abuses. A prominent contention of my article is that judges are the only people authorized to impose sentences and that prison officials are only authorized to impose necessary discipline. When prison officials impose extreme and prolonged disciplinary measures that are not justifiable for disciplinary or administrative purposes, prison officials, in effect, re-sentence a defendant (sometimes even to death). Because the administrative process often does not lend itself to meaningful substantive judicial oversight, courts are frequently unable to serve their function, which is to effect justice in such an instance where the lines of separation between branches have been impermissibly crossed. My article demonstrates how, if unchecked, this results in a situation where prison officials have more sentencing power than courts. And, worse, where prison officials use that power to silence voices they do not want heard or to remove influences they do not want dispersed amongst the prison population. Lastly, the article offers a suggested national legislative model for the periodic review process. This model attempts to rectify procedural and substantive shortcomings in the current review process.

I will briefly outline my research findings. It is my hope that you will read the work in its entirety and use it as a part of your committee's efforts and considerations.

<u>14th Amendment (Due Process Clause) and the Periodic Review Process</u>

The article offers the following insight relative to these topics:

As a result of there being no exact standards governing periodic review hearings, review hearings are in many instances nothing more than ritualistic exercises in formality. Often, the proceedings are hollow in that they do not genuinely probe into the suitability of an inmate's custody change, and they do not rule based on a measurable evidentiary standard. Many review hearings serve as veils for a predetermined decision to maintain an inmate in isolation on an indefinite or permanent basis. Further complicating the situation is the fact that judicial challenges to such proceedings may fall upon deaf ears because courts, concerned only with procedure and satisfied with the knowledge that a "process" was afforded, feel their work is done….[T]his does not comport with due process. Because inmates have no constitutional right to release from prolonged isolation, it is imperative they be afforded a just process when they are evaluated at periodic intervals….

<u>Separation of Powers</u>

On this issue, the article states:

As an extension of the executive, corrections administrators may not, according to the Doctrine of Separation of Powers, encroach upon the powers of the legislative or judicial branches of government. By design, a warden plays a very different role in the life of an inmate than does a sentencing judge, whose primary function it is to impose sentences. A sentencing judge has authority to remand a defendant to the custody of the corrections department. In most instances, a sentencing judge has no authority over how or where a defendant spends his time in custody. Once a defendant is taken into custody, his relationship with prison officials and administrators begin. What is important is the delineation of power between the two officials. Judges are not equipped with prison administrative authority and wardens are not equipped with sentencing authority. When prison officials impose pretextual and/or extreme and prolonged disciplinary or administrative measures that are not absolutely necessary for prison security purposes or genuinely connected to legitimate penological concerns, the prison official leaves the realm of discipline and enters the realm of sentencing/resentencing. In doing so, prison officials not only abuse their authority, but they assume authority they lack.

<u>Judicial Abstinence and the Potential for Abuses</u>

My article expresses:

Currently, there exists "a policy of minimum intrusion into the affairs of state prison administration" and a belief that state "prison officials . . . be vested with broad discretion . . ." With respect to inmate periodic review hearings, this often results in courts limiting their involvement to ensuring that inmates are afforded the process to which they are entitled. Often, courts will not evaluate or engage in a meaningful review of the process' substance.

*****

[O]ne might argue that, in the prison setting, courts have created a layer of immunity for prison officials, by refusing to scrutinize penal decision-making during the periodic review process. What is needed is a firm legal line….The legal line should memorialize the crossing point into too far. The challenge lies in stopping courts from enabling transgressions by prison officials with their silence, while at the same time ensuring that the courts are not put in the position of having to micromanage prison officials.

<u>Reform Proposal: Legislative Model for the Periodic Review Process</u>

My article advocates the following:

Conceding that prison officials must have liberal charge of an institution, this authority needs to be somewhat less absolute than it currently is. A lack of accountability or oversight corrupts as much as it serves to ratify innocent errors in judgment. The major reform advanced herein is that institutions should no longer have complete authority over decisions regarding inmates' exoduses from solitary confinement. As an alternative, a tiered approach should be implemented, whereby prison officials make the initial decision to place a prisoner in isolation and retain authority over the first periodic review, but where, thereafter, other eyes begin to watch, other ears begin to listen, and other minds begin to ponder the fate of the isolated inmate. This reform is consistent with the aspirations of the Supreme Court, which expressed that, in both civil and criminal proceedings, due process requires an "adjudicator who is not in [the] situation." In furtherance of this view, the Court has explained that "[e]ven an appeal and a trial de novo will not cure a failure to provide a neutral and detached adjudicator." Another significant proposed reform is that the process be regulated by actual legislation and not by the administrative rule-making process. The proposed model follows:

1. Preliminary Considerations

- This model is intended to have both prospective and retroactive application.
- This model assumes all players will be trained and informed, as a minimum, on the unique intricacies of penal institutions, solitary confinement, and due process.

2. Placement into Solitary Confinement

- Prison officials should maintain exclusive control over the process employed to place an inmate into solitary confinement.
- When being placed in solitary confinement, prisoners should know the reason for the placement and the duration of their sentence to solitary confinement, and should be provided with a case plan enumerating exactly what must be done to earn their exodus.
- Placement in solitary confinement as a result of perceptions that are not incident to actual actions or specific, actual, and legitimate security or penological concerns should be prohibited. Continued placement in solitary confinement based on dated security concerns should not be allowed.
- Prolonged solitary confinement should be abolished. However, the practice of reassigning an inmate to solitary confinement for a defined time, following an adverse review, should be allowed.
- Once in solitary confinement, inmates must have a means of defending their interests at review proceedings. They must have access to some programs and services so reformation can be established during the review process.

3. Periodic Reviews

- Reviews should be conducted at regular intervals. Four months is the recommendation.
- Burden of Proof: At every stage of the review process, the prison should bear the burden of showing: (1) that the case plan could be accomplished; and (2) how the inmate failed to satisfy the case plan.
- After completion of the first review, prison officials should no longer retain exclusive control over the review process.
- The initial review should be conducted by prison officials. If the decision is unfavorable, a seven-member special review board should be empaneled for all future reviews.
  The seven-member special review board should be comprised of:
  One ethicist or member of the clergy (to serve as Chair).
  One mental health professional or a social worker.
  One prisoner advocate or an exonerated person.
  One current academician.
  One former military leader or one former prison administrator.
  One former member of law enforcement.
  One lawyer (familiar with civil due process protections).
- The ethicist or clergy member should chair the board, as well as empanel the board from a pro bono list made available by professional organizations or by way of an official call for board volunteers.
- Members should not receive remuneration or anything of value in exchange for their service and should not be appointed by the prison. While having local members would be ideal, there

- would be no opposition to members from across jurisdictional lines. In fact, such would serve to promote national uniformity.
- Decisions should be made by the will of four members.

4. Periodic Review Determinations (by Prison Officials or by Special Review Board)

- The aim should be a determination of whether the inmate satisfied the case plan or if the inmate made a genuine attempt at satisfying the case plan.
- The inmate's release from confinement should be viewed on par with the prison administration's administrative and management concerns.
- The warden must articulate the penological interest at issue and present verifiable reasons for the placement request. The warden's views should be considered. The warden's statement should be treated as equal to the other evidence.
- Psychological evaluations should be an integral part of every review proceeding. They should be treated as equal to the other evidence.
- The inmate's disciplinary record should be an integral part of every review proceeding. It should be treated as equal to the other evidence. The absence of recent infractions should be persuasive, but not outcome determinative.
- Release denials should require a short statement of reasons for continued confinement, as well as articulation of future release criteria in the form of a supplemental case plan.
- Decisions should be made upon a showing of a preponderance of actual evidence to justify keeping a person in isolation. Said evidence should establish that the prisoner "poses a credible continuing and serious threat to the security of others or to the prisoner's own safety."
- Expert opinions may be considered during the review process. If used, they should be treated as equal to the other evidence.

5. Court's Role in the Review Process

The review should extend to the procedure afforded, as well as to the merits of the adverse finding. When reviewing the merits, the aim should be a determination of whether the inmate satisfied the case plan or if the inmate made a genuine attempt at satisfying the case plan.

When reviewing the merits, courts should ensure:

The burden of proof was met.

The inmate's release from confinement was viewed on par with the prison administration's administrative and management concerns.

Due process was afforded. This means that:

a. Substantively, the inmate had the opportunity to show that no credible continuing and serious threat to the security of others or to the prisoner's own safety exists.

b. A sincere effort was made at determining if the inmate satisfied or genuinely attempted to satisfy the case plan.

c. The current punishment is connected to a current security concern and not a dated one.

d. The current punishment is connected to a legitimate security threat and not a perceived one.

e. The decision was made upon a showing of a preponderance of actual evidence establishing that the prisoner poses a credible continuing and serious threat to the security of others or to the prisoner's own safety.

After six periodic reviews (under the same case/issue), judicial review may be sought by any aggrieved party (prison official or the inmate).

The late Professor Derrick Bell spoke these insightful words:

> Telling the truth can be hard and even painful work, but lying, keeping the truth secret, is far more painful. When we think lying isn't hard and painful, it's rarely because its become easy and pleasant; more likely it's because we have put up a wall between ourselves and our awareness of our captivity. This is why I am surprised that so few people in difficulty fail to tell the truth when confronted with conduct that is dishonest or less than honorable—even when admitting that conduct could lead to civil liability or criminal prosecution….Generally, though, the truth will come out; when it does, chances are that you will be worse off for having dissembled, evaded, or out-and-out lied.

> On the question of how solitary confinement is being used in America's penal institutions, truth is our serum and our magic portion. We must drink of it and we must generously pass the cup. For too long, the truth has been silenced, withheld and suppressed where solitary confinement is concerned. We must now be liberated by this truth. And after our work of exposing the truth is done, we must not recline or delight in a sense of accomplishment. Meaningful change must follow, lest we become victims of inertia.

> Incarceration by its very nature invites condescension toward and perhaps even disdain for inmates. But it offers no reason or excuse to diminish the rights or the humanity of the incarcerated. Affording justice to inmates does not and should not depend on the good faith or forbearance of prison officials. It is mandated by our form of government. Mindless insistence on maintaining order in prisons without concern for the rights of inmates is antipodal to democracy.

An additional way of participating is speaking before legislative committees as bills are considered. Ed Tarply was one of the people to perform this role when ending non-unanimous juries was before lawmakers.[40] I offer these suggestions for those wishing to present before a legislative body:

<u>Preparation</u>:

- What you will say should be written. I suggest two versions: (1) one that is available for public review; and, (2) a private copy that is in bullet format to be used as a reference during the oral presentation.
- Find the time limitations in advance and tailor your remarks accordingly. Three to five minutes is typical.
- It's a good idea to prepare by reviewing prior hearings (by accessing the archives). When a committee meeting is in progress, the words "In Progress" appears next to the name of the committee and clicking that link will take you to the live video broadcast. You can also view certain prior archived committee meetings via the House's archived video repository or the Senate's archived video repository.

<u>As you draft</u>:

- Remember that legislators entertain thousands of bills, most outside their area of expertise. Their days are full. What's most helpful to them are messages that avoid technical language, jargon and volume. Aim for clarity and conciseness.
- Think like you are drafting a "for sale" advertisement. Say a lot in a few words. Use persuasive language so the "buyer" can see the benefits of buying your "product" and the disadvantages and risks associated with the other "products." Don't underestimate the intelligence of the committee. Don't overestimate their knowledge either.
- If you are collaborating with others, consult with the group and divide topics to ensure all important points are covered and to minimize the possibility of repetition.
- Anticipate and plan for questions during or after your testimony.

- Don't try to cover every aspect of the issue. Settle on one or two angles and address just that.
- Only use a visual aid if it will have a greater impact than words, i.e. chart, diagram, photo.
- The introduction should: (1) state your full name and official title and/or group affiliation (if applicable); (2) your connection to the issue; (3) the bill you are speaking about; and, (4) your position, i.e. in favor/in opposition/presenting information.
- The body should: (1) tell the committee exactly why this change/no change is good for the people of Louisiana; (2) tell the committee the benefits that will result from them acting upon your advice; (3) tell the committee of the harms and dangers that will come to the public if they don't act upon your advice; and, (4) use personal stories and accounts as much as possible.
- The conclusion should: (1) state what you want in clear terms; (2) announce your availability for questions; and, (3) thank the committee for considering your position.
- Review the script many times so you are confident and ready to present in conversational form on the day of the hearing.
- Print many copies. Sometimes legislators have overlapping hearings. If they miss your oral testimony, be ready to give them a hardcopy to read.

<u>Once at the hearing</u>:

- Arrive early.
- See the Sergeant-at-Arms or committee secretary to ascertain a copy of the <u>required</u> witness card (or you will not be allowed to speak).

HOUSE WITNESS CARD-AFFIRMATION

Committee: _____________   Date: ___________

Regarding: HB No: ______   HCR No: ______   HR No: ______
SB No: ______   SCR No: ______   Other: _________

Check one:

☐ I am present & would like to speak
☐ I am present & will provide information, if requested
☐ Although I do not wish to speak, I am present & in support

Please Print:
Name: _______________   Primary Telephone: ______________
Representing: _______________   Cell: _____________
Address: _______________   Email: _____________

I hereby affirm that the written or oral testimony I give before this committee will be true and correct. By ascribing my signature below, I acknowledge that I will be giving sworn testimony under oath, and that any intentional false statement material to the matter or issue before this committee is a violation of that oath.

Signature of Witness: ______________________

Witness cards come in three colors:

Green: For those speaking in support of a bill.

Red: For those speaking in opposition to a bill.

White: For those wishing to simply provide information.

HOUSE WITNESS CARD - AFFIRMATION * IN OPPOSITION

Committee: _______________   Date: ___________
Regarding: HB No. ________   HCR No. _______   HR No. _______
SB No. ________   SCR No. ________   Other: _______

CHECK ONE:
[ ] I am present and would like to speak
[ ] I am present and will provide information, if requested
[ ] Although I do not wish to speak, I am present and in opposition

PLEASE PRINT:
Name: _________________________
Representing: _________________________
Address: _________________________

Primary telephone: (   ) ____________   Cell: (   ) ____________
e-mail address: _________________________

I hereby affirm that the written or oral testimony I give before this committee will be true and correct. By ascribing my signature below, I acknowledge that I will be giving sworn testimony, under oath, and that any intentional false statement material to the matter or issue before this committee is a violation of that oath.

Signature of Witness: _________________________

The witness card requires a signature affirming that the testimony is true and correct.[41] During the presentation, the speaker is considered under oath.[42]

COVID-19 prompted many states to hold remote hearings. In those settings, the opportunity to request to speak and also register an opinion on a bill or to submit written testimony was done electronically. This online process may continue in certain jurisdictions. Even before the pandemic, Alaska, Nevada, New York, Washington and Wyoming used websites to gather constituent feedback on specific bills or special topics. Consult your jurisdiction to see if these options exist there.

- Come with patience and time allocated for a wait. Hearings can be delayed or the order of bills can change. Once the hearing begins, the committee doesn't adhere to a first come, first served approach. Instead, public officials are often allowed to testify first.
- Have the paper remarks as a guide, but don't read. Maintain good eye contact with each committee member. The most impactful testimony is conversational and heartfelt.
- Respect time limitations. If you don't, expect the committee chair to ask you to conclude.
- If questions are presented, it is appropriate to state that you can't answer if the question exceeds the scope of your knowledge or expertise. Credibility is very important. Don't offer information that you are not sure about. It's also appropriate to agree to supplement your response with further documentation after the hearing if you can't provide a sound or complete response at the time.
- Be respectful and diplomatic. Some hearings are emotional. Be sure to exercise restraint in the face of challenges or differing opinions. Use research, statistics, sound reasoning or other pervasive strategies to respond, but never allow emotions to drive responses.
- Display cultural literacy. Consider the way your words will impact those who hear them, which means the

committee, those present in the room, those viewing by video and those who will see the video later.

If only Calcasieu Parish District Attorney John DeRosier had read this book before his April 2018 appearance before the House Criminal Justice Committee to express his opposition to changing Louisiana's law to a unanimous jury system. He expressed concerns that requiring unanimous verdicts could result in more mistrials–slowing down the judicial process because cases would have to be heard again. He urged members of the committee to consider more than the history of the law when they vote.

DeRosier continued, "I've heard a lot about this system being adopted as a result of a vestige of slavery....I'm not proud of that... But it is what it is." Representatives Ted James and Denise Marcelle expressed the collective devastation felt by many spectators and legislators. "We can agree to disagree but what we can't do is sit here and be insulted by saying it is what it is about racism," Marcelle said. Representative James expressed "To admit that it started in slavery and to say 'it is what it is.' I am utterly offended."

- Respect the environment. The process calls for professional decorum, such as silence as others present, civility towards opponents and restraint from outbursts during or after the hearing.
- Understand "the process before the process." As explained by former legislator J. P. Morrell, "In the legislature, every vote is pretty much pre-decided. When you go to the floor of the senate or the house, you have the votes before the vote or you don't...."[43]

<u>Post-Hearing:</u>

- Bearing the above in mind, after the hearing, it is appropriate to thank committee members for their attention to your concerns by email, card or letter.
- After the hearing, it is appropriate to furnish committee members with follow-up responses to questions that you agreed to provide.

Public presence at hearings can have tremendous impact so filling the hearing room is an important part of advocacy before the legislature. Hearings don't replace or render useless in-person visits with legislators. Citizens can avail themselves to these in-person visits in the same way lobbyists can. In some states and in congress, staff members have great influence over legislative decision-making so don't be disappointed if you meet with a staff member instead of your legislator. Use this link to find out who your state and federal legislators are: https://legis.la.gov/legis/findmylegislators.aspx .

To remain connected with the work of committees of interest, you can sign up for free email notifications of future committee meetings (by using this link: https://legis.la.gov/legis/meetingnotifica tions.aspx). The notice will include links to the specific committee agenda.

An additional way of participating in the legislative process is through direct communication with legislators, either via personal conversation, email or letter. Louisiana State Representative and former Chairman of the Louisiana Legislative Black Caucus, Vincent Pierre feels especially impacted by direct communications:

> As elected officials, our days can be consumed with so much state business that deciphering and recalling significant details on a range of issues can be challenging. When I'm sitting in my office or at home reviewing the day's documents and I come across

letters from constituents where they share the intimate particulars of their situation with pleas for assistance or words of appreciation, I draw in and grasp tightly to their words. They're what keep me up at night coordinating available resources to provide assistance, or they are reminders to me to keep fighting the good fight...it is their written words that remind me why I became a representative, which is solely to serve and respond to the needs of the people of Louisiana.

The legislative process can end in the creation or modification of law or nothing more than the start of a conversation that yielded no immediate results. Sometimes the result is a hearing, study, report and/or resolution that further evaluates an issue with no definite commitments attached. An example of this is found in Phase III of the non-unanimous jury campaign. Instead of getting the desired law that could address those persons whose non-unanimous jury convictions were final (those who fell under the *Edwards v. Vannoy* litigation), a resolution was achieved.[44]

It created the 2021 "Equal Justice Task Force," to formulate "a method to enable the judicial system of Louisiana and the DPSC to ensure the equal application of laws as such laws relate to individuals who may have been subjected to a miscarriage of justice due to the non-unanimous jury verdict law in Louisiana."

After all this effort, there can also be a law that goes unimplemented, which VOTE Policy Counsel Will Harrell says, "isn't worth the paper it is written on." When you do this work, you must understand the range of possibilities and be open to reasonable delays and compromises that are not detrimental to the ultimate objective.

Boards, Councils and Commissions

Local boards, councils and commissions are an important part of policy and law work. These are also the bodies that most directly impact the daily lives of citizens. As is the case with the legislature, the process at these local bodies also allow for public participation. Rules also govern these processes. Their rules must be followed. Advocates must not overlook the importance of these spaces.

If advocacy work is specific to justice-impacted populations, pardon and parole boards should be considered in this same vein. The board is not there to heal your heart. They are there for one reason: to protect the public. That's the burden you must be prepared to meet. Carefully select speakers who are credible. Speakers who hold the public trust are best. Make sure every speaker explains how public safety won't be compromised by the release of the person. The following things might be persuasive:

- A demonstration of a good conduct record while incarcerated (and no recent write ups).
- The ability to show that all programming has been taken advantage of, such as school, therapy, self-help classes, etc.
- A demonstration of a conversion behind bars.
- Demonstrating that time behind bars has been used constructively and toward improvement.
- Remorse for the act that led to incarceration.
- Empathy for any victims, which includes the family of the justice-impacted person, the community and the person impacted by the criminal act.
- A suitable housing and employment plan.
- Low risk of criminal conduct post-release.

Pleas from loved ones are not useless, but, are rarely persuasive in the absence of the above.

A Consequence Plan

This final advocacy strategy may not appear at first blush, to be a strategy, but it absolutely is. Every advocate should consult with a legal advisor at regular intervals to ensure the legality of actions and to assess the consequences. Change agents must have a plan in place for any civil litigation or criminal changes that arise. This should be done in advance of the litigation or charge. That plan should include legal representation and a means to pay for any costs associated with it or with arrest. If the advocacy involves groups of citizens, the same applies.

For example, during the civil rights era, a bail fund was established in advance of direct action. When change agents were arrested, these funds were used to post bail and secure their release. GoFundMe is not as certain as a bail fund, but it has been used successfully in recent times. Reggie Ray is infamously known for using a chair to strike one of the aggressors in the Montgomery, Alabama 2023 riverfront, racial attack upon a dock worker. After Ray was arrested for disorderly conduct, his attorney set up a GoFundMe to support his release and representation. Within days, over $260,000 in donations were given. This is an option to consider, but the uncertainties should be fully understood and contemplated.

CONCLUSION

In 1792, Captain John Kimber was tried by a British jury for the death of a 14-year-old Black girl who died at his hands during transport aboard *The Recovery*. She had earlier been kidnapped from Africa. Those aboard were shackled together and crammed tightly into the crevasses of the ship. The young girl was weak and lethargic. She, along with some other females, were suffering the effects of untreated gonorrhea amongst other maladies. As Captain Kimber transported his enslaved passengers, he made a customary request of his human cargo. The captives were commanded to dance. The young girl did not comply.

Captain Kimber became frustrated by her refusal. He suspended her in the air and administered an unmerciful beating with a whip. He stopped and ordered an enslaved male to pull her legs with a sudden jerk. He complied. The beating continued over a prolonged period. According to the record:

> She remained suspended for about five minutes. During that time,
> she was bounced up and down, or in other words, lifted up, and

let fall again...She was then taken down and suspended in the same manner by the other arm. She was next lifted up by one leg; and afterwards by the other until at last she was taken up for the fifth time by both hands, and underwent the fifth excruciating suspension. The whole time from the first to the last suspension, this witness said might have been half an hour. While she continued hung up by both hands, the prisoner lashed her inhumanly with his whip: and when she was let down, he forced her to walk without any assistance down the hatchway: this she was unable to do, having got but two or three steps, when she slipped... she was welted in several parts of the body, her hands were swelled in consequence of the hanging, and her legs disfigured in a shocking manner: after this the witness saw her in convulsions, had her brought on deck, and rubbed her with volatile spirits; but every remedy was ineffectual: she languished away in this miserable state for three days, and-on the third expired.

Captain Kimber was not convicted. Another book might discuss what the legal system failed to do to him. But not this one. This moment belongs to the nameless 14-year-old girl. I declare her the lead actress in this story—the alpha and the omega. She was likely doing a visioning exercise that day. She likely imagined what she wanted to transition to. In resisting, she demanded a new thing. You are the distance between her and achievement of that new thing.

You are hereby summoned to duty!

ACKNOWLEDGMENTS

This book signals the end of a journey inspired by my days working inside the judiciary and from my work on the "underground railroad to justice" for over twenty years. After witnessing, breathing and ingesting what justice means to many players in the legal system, I realized there was a wide gap between what law school taught me about the legal system, what the ABA aspires, what citizens believe about the legal system they trust and what the legal system really is and, most importantly, what it is not. This book is my feeble attempt at arming lawyers and non-lawyers with some tools for achieving victories in the existing legal system, as well as doing the work of transitioning to a new system.

In 2020, I was selected as the speaker for the distinguished Charles Frye Memorial Lecture at S.U. at New Orleans (SUNO).

That 2020 keynote address, *When Law & Injustice Became Bedfellows, Justice Becomes the Business of the People*, served as the first part of a two-part effort to enlighten lawyers and non-lawyers about the shortcomings of the legal system and to arm them with some of the extrajudicial tools needed to interface with the legal system (or any other system that harms) and/or to do the work of systemic transformation.

Dr. Clyde Robertson, Director of African and African American Studies at SUNO & Angela A. Allen-Bell.

The second event was advocacy training for both lawyers and non-lawyers. The response was so overwhelming, the program had to be moved to a larger venue in order to accommodate the demand. That was confirmation that the public needed training to work in conjunction with lawyers or in lieu of them. It also demonstrated a collective appetite for both justice and transition.

Since that *"Disrupting the Injustice Narrative"* training, I have continued to receive communications and calls from lawyers and non-lawyers alike requesting help navigating the complicated world of systemic change or who simply need to survive a bout with the current legal system. These conversations became confirmation for the efforts undertaken by me between then and now. In reflection, I can only now appreciate the way these two events and the many communications they prompted led to the development and completion of this book. I extend a heartfelt gesture of appreciation to Dr. Clyde Robertson for his many years of sage advice, for his novel insights, for the respect and support he extends to fellow activists and thought-leaders and for his enthusiasm and zealous partnership during this two-part program.

Agreeing to write a book under the circumstances that I wrote meant simultaneously agreeing to temporarily absent myself from the people and things that matter most. This project consumed the hours I was not teaching or sleeping. Having a support team in life is not something I take for granted. My team includes my two daughters and my husband of thirty-two years. I cherish the three of you and thank you for the sacrificial spirit you have all shown throughout this process. I am also profoundly grateful to each of you for your editorial and technical contributions. My team also includes K-9 companions Drama, Bailey and Justice, my walking and office mates, who bring me immeasurable joy. They took occupancy at the window near my desk and were tortured by the presence of squirrels and birds that they could not chase as I wrote. Let the games begin again!

My village understood years of autoreplies, unanswered calls and emails, my unavailability for partnerships and my failure to attend events during this period. It took this for me to finish. I am immensely grateful for the understanding and support. You know I am speaking of you if you have secretly wished I stop sending all those dog photos, social justice emails and text messages. Beyond the above, there is a village of friends, comrades, allies and family (both through birth and marriage) that sustains and supports me and keeps me grounded. Lisa, Regina, Monica and Kacy, you are the best girlfriends the world has to offer. You never compete, envy or judge. You only love, support and call me out on those very rare instances when it is needed. Angola 3 member Robert King, members of the Louisiana Alumni Chapter of the Black Panther Party, Students United, attorney Ernest Jones, attorney Willie Zanders, Sr. and Calvin Duncan, I'm watching your moves and trying my best to emulate them. I leave every conversation with you improved and wiser.

I thank SULC for the award of summer writing stipends used to partially fund my summer research endeavors and the Culture of Health Leadership Institute for Racial Healing for the award of partial summer funds and for enriching content that inspired hope in the ideas advanced in this book. Writing books of this nature and pursuing the scholarship and path of an activist scholar is not something that every law professor is created to do and it is not something they are all free to live. I pay homage to SULC for never devaluing scholarship that contradicts or questions prevailing themes in law. And it is in this sacred space that I have met some of the most talented future lawyers in the country (many of whom are now impactful lawyers around the country). Working with this population of students completes me. Many of these students encouraged this work. Their words carried me many days.

My gratitude to Anne Sobol (relative to her late husband Richard Sobol) and Tiffany Rainey for their contribution of time, insights and content. A final extension of gratitude is given to all those unnamed teachers and persons who poured into me, counseled me, prayed and encouraged me through this process and over the years leading up to it. Your presence has been felt and has been consequential. You are my sustenance.

POST-SCRIPT

This post-script serves as my response to those desiring suggested areas of immediate attention and/or for those seeking to confront shortcomings during transition of the legal system. They are:

Redress for Victims of Non-Unanimous Juries Who Remain in Custody

The SCOTUS recognized Louisiana's authority to fashion a solution for the men and women who remain in custody because of non-unanimous juries. Louisiana must accept this responsibility because these men and women did not get convicted through a credible process. This work awaits.

Credible Bias and Cultural Literacy Training Programs

Bias and cultural humility training should be mandatory for every person involved with the carceral state. The training should be uniform and the content of that training should not be left to the discretion of the various agencies, departments or trainers. The training program should be meaningful, which means a vetting process for trainers is warranted. Trainers should be published and credentialed experts on race and bias. And judges must begin to act boldly in response to bias and racism as did Justice Lemmon when a prosecutor who stuck Black jurors said, in a closing argument before an all-white jury, that they not let the O.J. Simpson prototype "[get] away with it." Justice Lemmon responded that "Racially inflammatory tactics, such as [this]...should not be tolerated, even at the expense of the reversal of convictions and sentences obtained by their use...."[1] There are also some laudable local and other recent efforts by the ABA, but they are still inadequate.[2] This work awaits.

Removal of Supremacist and/or Offensive Words, Images and/or Structures

Thought must be given to spaces where justice is served and communicated. What's displayed in or outside of courthouses or in legal texts can convey harmful messages to the accused, witnesses, jurors or others. The Daughters of the Confederacy, founded in 1894, have played a prominent role in preserving the supremacist regime of the South. They worked with the KKK to maintain supremacy in the South and have been integral in erecting monuments and statutes to commemorate Confederate generals. They claimed their efforts as preservationist in nature, but they were intended to downplay the realities surrounding the Civil War.

Years ago, attorney Niles Haymer started demanding that Confederate monuments be removed from outside Louisiana courthouses. The thought of celebrating a treasonous government that it took a war to overthrow offends him and many others. He implored the Louisiana State Bar Association and the Louisiana Supreme Court to provide leadership on this issue. He lamented, "These monuments don't belong where people of all races go to seek justice, fairness and equality, because we all can agree that the Confederacy never stood for that."[3]

By extension, change agents should focus efforts on the removal of supremacist or offensive words from laws and removing images and/or structures that lack objectivity in judicial spaces. This effort should rid laws of proxy words or words that affirm racial hierarchies and replace them with terms of solidarity. Words that encourage false narratives should be replaced also. Instead of labeling people, words that speak of them situationally should be used. Language that dehumanize or blame people instead of the system that created the problem should be avoided. For example, slave v. enslaved our houseless v homeless.

Language that reinforces racial hierarchies or white supremacy should be changed. Shockingly, some of the civil rights statutes do this by using "white citizens" as the metric for equality. For example, Section 1981 of Title 42, adopted as part of the Civil Rights Act of 1866, provides "All persons within the jurisdiction of the United States shall have the same right in every State and Territory to make and enforce contracts, to sue, be parties, give evidence, and to the full and equal benefit of all laws and proceedings for the security of persons and property as is enjoyed *by white citizens . . . .*" This work awaits.

<u>Require Open File Discovery</u>

Louisiana should require open file discovery by the prosecution, as many states already do. This allows defense counsel access to information in the prosecution files, such as police reports and eyewitness testimonies without the barrier of having to file requests for exculpatory information. This has the added benefit of speeding up the trial process. It is a reform long advocated by the IPNO. This work awaits.

<u>Broadening the Scope of Voir Dire</u>

Voir dire should be broadened to allow defendants of color to explore matters of racial prejudice during jury selection. This work awaits.

Mandate Trauma-Informed Training

A traumatic event renders a person's internal and external resources inadequate, leaving them unable to effectively cope. Trauma-informed judges, lawyers, police, legislators, probation officers and teachers recognize the signs of trauma and understand that it manifests itself through a range of emotional and physical symptoms, including reconfiguring the brain, depression, anxiety, hopelessness, explosive reactions and avoidance, among other things. Having this training allows judges, probation officers, prison administrators, school disciplinarians, lawmakers and criminal justice players to recognize trauma and to fashion solutions, punishments and outcomes with this in mind. This work awaits.

Attention to Emotional Justice

The intangible work of learning new ways of relating to each other and of confronting personal traumas is a central part of reform. The American Institute of Emotional Justice (AIEJ) identifies emotional justice (EJ) as "the roadmap for racial healing" because of the way it "connects us to the role of the emotional in oppressive systems that harm and shape us, and sustain systemic inequity."[4] EJ looks to "the emotional work that white and Black people need to do to end systemic inequity."

AIEJ explains that emotional work as "exploring, identifying and severing the connections in our relationship to power and race that uphold systemic inequity by unlearning the language of whiteness."[5] Emotions educator Yolo Akili explains the importance of prioritizing EJ during a period of transition:

> Oppression is trauma. Every form of inequity has a traumatic impact on the psychology, emotionality and spiritu-

ality of the oppressed. The impact of oppressive trauma creates cultural and individual wounding. This wounding becomes an impediment to the individual and collective's ability to transform and negotiate their conditions. EJ... find[s] ways to transform our collective and individual pains into power...It calls on us to not just speak to why something is problematic, but to speak to the emotional texture of how it impacts us; how it hurts, or how it brings us joy or nourishment. [6]

As this work is done, Yolo encourages freedom of emotional expression where people are allowed to address their pain as they feel the need.[7] Yolo warns, "Our patriarchal emotional discourses will push back against this...and will instead encourage us to deny, dismiss, and move on as quickly as possible from difficult emotions."[8] "Engaging emotional justice requires us to check this attitude within ourselves and develop ongoing strategies that allow us to express our concerns and feelings."[9] This work awaits.

Ban Facial Recognition Technology

Because of bias in the algorithms used, facial recognition technology is unreliable. It has caused a disproportionate number of Black people to be falsely arrested. Some states have banned or restricted the use of this technology by the police and other public agencies or businesses. This work awaits.

Addressing Jury Diversity/Jury Underrepresentation

The underrepresentation of jurors of color is driven by the strategic exclusion of minorities from jury pools and during the selection process, legal barriers to jury participation and misconceptions about jury duty that discourage participation. None of these challenges are insurmountable. This work awaits.

Juror Strikes

Too many jurors of color are struck from juries because lawyers circumvent the current law. Some states have adopted legislation to guard against this. Louisiana has not. This work awaits.

Wrongful Convictions

Despite the progress realized, IPNO director Jee Park says, "Louisiana's wrongful conviction compensation and loss of life payment to innocent exonerees is woefully inadequate." Park continues, "Innocent exonerees are deprived of the most productive years of their lives by no fault of their own and because, on average, they win their freedom well after their prime working years, they are left with no savings, investments and social security benefits." Because, according to Park, many Louisiana exonerees "struggle to pay for their basic needs and support their loved ones," further reforms are warranted. This work awaits.

The Death Penalty

There are racial disparities surrounding the imposition of death sentences. There's also the reality that Louisiana imposes the sentence, but often fails to actually put people to death. Given both, is it time to eliminate this sentencing option? This work awaits.

The Exceptions Clause

Louisiana's constitution mirrors the federal constitution in allowing for slavery and involuntary servitude once a person is in custody following a conviction. Governing documents should not provide justification for slavery or servitude. The constitution should be amended. I endorse labor that can help reintegrate a person into society or that can incentivize behavior modifications so I oppose an outright ban on work for those in custody. In 2018, Colorado became the first state since Rhode Island in 1842 to ban slavery and involuntary servitude outright. Two years after a failed attempt to change their law, Coloradans voted 66% to 34% for an amendment reading: "There shall never be in this state either slavery or involuntary servitude." Utah and Nebraska removed the language in 2020. Language consistent with Colorado's is what I advocate.[10]

Greater Use of Posthumous Pardons

The Avery C. Alexander Act, authored by former Louisiana State Senator Edwin Murray of New Orleans, created an expedited application process for posthumous pardons. It has only been used once (in the case of the late Homer Plessy). Additional work in this arena awaits.

Placing Limits on the Use of Social Media & Art During Trials

The use of social media posts and/or creative expression as criminal evidence against a person without clear and convincing proof that there is a literal, factual nexus between the post or creative expression and the facts of the case must end. Louisiana's recently enacted Rap Act fails to offer sufficient protections to the accused. This work awaits.

Modifying the Judicial Complaints Process

Greater judicial transparency is needed when complaints are filed with the Judiciary Commission of Louisiana.[11] A sitting judge can be reelected with open complaints and the public has no way of knowing those complaints are pending. This work awaits.

Confronting Prosecutorial Misconduct

At least three changes should be considered to minimize the instances of prosecutorial misconduct in the transitioned justice system. Immunity is first. Immunity must end or be modified. Criminal charges must be considered for prosecutors who violate the law.[12] A third reform involves discipline for offending prosecutors. Under a transitioned system, the pursuit of discipline against reported prosecutors would look very different and the court's response to these transgressions would change also.

Currently, the disciplinary process is not addressing prosecutorial misconduct. Some would even argue, by its record of inaction, it is encouraging it. There are reasons that should be considered during the reform process. Sometimes citizens, lawyers, and justice-impacted people don't report misconduct. Judges, many of whom were themselves former prosecutors, also fail to address or report misconduct that they witness or discover in proceedings.

Perhaps, they have unknowingly become desensitized to the point when the conduct is seen, but no longer noticed. With no report to the ODC, nothing can be done to address prosecutorial misconduct from the standpoint of the state bar. Then, there are instances where reports are made, but inaction or insufficient action follows. Efforts such as an attempt to create a legislative remedy in the form of a State Commission on Prosecutorial Oversight, a State Commission on Prosecutorial Conduct and the Code of Prosecutorial Conduct have been stalled. These and other prosecutorial misconduct reforms are badly in need of attention.

What's presented is not an exclusive listing. It's merely an attempt to inspire thought about future priorities. I discourage what I term "the buffet approach to social change." Often, at a buffet style meal, the inclination is to overindulge at the sight of an abundance of palate-pleasing options. The consumer loads the plate with more than their stomach has the capacity to comfortably hold. Either they can't consume all of what they select or they consume it and get sick. For those who accept the summons, the same can happen so be mindful of portion control. Not only is the portioned entrée better for your health and well-being than a smorgasbord of options from the buffet, the entrée is also better for the overall cause of change because working in a focused way is the only pathway to successful change.

NOTES

Introduction

1. Restorative justice is "an approach to remedying crime in which it is understood that all things are interrelated and that crime disrupts the harmony which existed prior to its occurrence, or at least which it is felt should exist. The appropriateness of a particular sanction is largely determined by the needs of the victims, and the community, as well as the offender. The focus is on the human beings closely affected by the crime." *R. v. Gladue*, 1999 CanLII 679, 71 (SCC).

2. Transitional justice refers to "formal attempts by post repressive or post conflict societies to address past wrongdoing in their effort to democratize." Colleen Murphy, *The Conceptual Foundations of Transitional Justice* 1 (2017). There are five pillars to a TJ model that complement and reinforce each other: (1) truth-seeking; (2) memorialization; (3) prosecutions/justice; (4) reparations; and, (5) legal and policy reforms/the guarantee of non-recurrence. These five pillars are interrelated. Each ensures the success of the next and they all collectively ensure the success of the transition.

3. The Reconstruction Amendments' Debates (Alfred Avins ed, 2nd ed. 1974) (38th Cong., 1st Sess. 44 (Feb. 29, 1864) (Statement of Charles Sumner).

4. La. Const. art I, § 1.

5. Civil law jurisdictions have legal codes that specify all matters capable of being brought before a court, the applicable procedure, and the appropriate punishment for each offense. In a civil law system, the judge's role is to establish the facts of the case and to apply the provisions of the applicable code. The judge's decision is consequently less crucial in shaping civil law than the decisions of legislators and legal scholars who draft and interpret the codes.

6. Secretary-General's message on the International Day for the Elimination of Racial Discrimination, March 21, 2022.

7. *See* CERD/C/USA/CO/10-12, *Concluding observations on the Combined tenth to twelfth reports of the United States of America*, United Nations (2022), *available at* tbinternet.ohchr.org/_layouts/15/treatybodyexternal/Download.aspx?symbolno=CERD%2FC%2FUSA%2FCO%2F10-12&Lang=en (last visited July 4, 2023).

8. "Freedom, by definition, is people realizing that they are their own leaders." (Diane Nash); "Power concedes nothing without a demand. It never did and it never will." (Frederick Douglass); "The way to right wrongs is to turn the light of truth upon them." (Ida B. Wells); "If a law is unjust, a man is not only right to disobey it, he is obligated to do so." (Thomas Jefferson); "Get up, stand up, Stand up for your rights. Get up, stand up, Don't give up the fight." (Bob

Marley); "Disobedience is the true foundation of liberty. The obedient must be slaves." (Henry David Thoreau); "I am no longer accepting the things I cannot change. I am changing the things I cannot accept." (Angela Davis); "When you see something that is not just, not fair, or not right, you have to do something. You have to say something. Make a little noise. It's time for us to get into good trouble, necessary trouble." (John Lewis).

9. This statement is subject to the laws in the jurisdiction within which transition is attempted.

Chapter 1

1. Official Journal of the Proceedings of the Constitutional Convention of the State of Louisiana, pp. 36 (1898).
2. Jennifer A. Goodson, *A Citizen's Guide to Advocacy*, World Vision, *available at* A-Citizens-Guide-to-Advocacy.pdf (worldvision.org) (last visited July 23, 2024).
3. Robin D. G. Kelley, Freedom Dreams: The Black Radical Imagination 28 (2022).
4. Matiangai Sirleaf and E. Tendayi Achiume, *Reflecting on Race, Racism and Transitional Justice,* 18 The International Journal of Transitional Justice, 1, 17 (March 2024).
5. *See* Angela A. Allen-Bell, *Under Indictment: Race, Juries & Justice in Louisiana* 27-30 (2024).
6. *See Strategic Action Plan Report of the Secretary-General's Task Force on Addressing Racism and Promoting Dignity for All in the United Nations Secretariat,* at 7 (2021) (citing foreword by Catherine Pollard Under-Secretary-General for Management Strategy, Policy and Compliance).
7. *Id.*
8. Gail C. Christopher, *Px Racial Healing A Guide to Embracing our Humanity xiii* (2022).
9. *See* Khiara M. Bridges, *Critical Race Theory A Primer* 195 (2019).
10. *See Id.*
11. Just Lead Washington, *Washington Pro Bono Equity Training Guide: Race Equity & Cultural Competency Curriculum for Volunteer Lawyers*, p. 14, *available at* Washington Pro Bono Equity Training Guide: Race Equity & Cultural Competency Curriculum for Volunteer Lawyers (justleadwa.org) (last visited March 8, 2022).
12. *Id.*
13. *Id.*
14. Maxine Crump invites the public to connect with DORLA by visiting their website (dialogueonracelouisiana.org).
15. Gyimah invites the public to connect with AMOA on their social media platforms (Facebook, Instagram, and YouTube) or by visiting their website (www.theamoa.org).

16. *See* Janel George, *A Lesson on Critical Race Theory*, ABA 46 Human Rights Magazine 2, Jan. 11, 2021, *available at* A Lesson on Critical Race Theory (americanbar.org) (last visited May 31, 2022).

17. *Id.*

18. *Id.*

19. *Id.*

20. *Id.*

21. *Id.*

22. Glorida J. Brown-Marshall, *She Took Justice the Black Woman, Law and Power 1619 to 1969* 42 (2021).

23. *Id.*

24. Race & Slavery Petitions Project, *available at* Petition Details (uncg.edu)https://library.uncg.edu/slavery/petitions/details.aspx?pid=6903 (last visited May 7, 2021)(discussing two enslaved men who responded to attempts by the overseer to administer beatings by once striking the overseer with an axe, leaving his hand "in a most awkward manner" and the other attacking the overseer with a club and a knife that "nearly severed the little finger."; In 1810, Azi was convicted of assault and battery upon his master and sentenced to hang with a description of the crime written on his back. Criminal Case File no. 167, a complaint against Negro Azi, a slave of Josef, 1810, *available at* Criminal case file no. 167, Complaint against the Negro Azi, a slave of Joseph, 1810 - Criminal case file no. 167, Complaint against the Negro Azi, a slave of Joseph, 1810 | Louisiana Digital Library (last visited May 7, 2021).

25. Judah, a fourteen-year-old enslaved girl, confessed to poisoning three of her owner's children and attempting to burn her owner's Maryland plantation house down. One child died in the fire. Two others died as a result of the poisoning. In 1831, a death sentence was imposed. *See* Gail Thomas, Kenvi Phillips & Stacey Shorter, *A Brief History African-American Historic and Cultural Resource*, 45 (2012), *available at* African-Americans in Prince George's County.pdf (last visited Feb, 21, 2022).

26. For example, Louisiana is site to the 1812 Slave Revolt and the Lafayette Parish Slave Rebellion of 1840; In 1791, Toussaint L'ouverture organized a revolution in an effort to stop the enslavement of Africans in France. At the end of the Haitian Revolution, the French were ultimately defeated by Toussaint L'Ouverture and the people of African descent who fought with him for years. The Africans beat trained military troops from Britain, Span and France. They ultimately succeed in the creation of the independent nation of Haiti. Haiti is the first independent Black nation in the Western Hemisphere.

27. *See Back v Meeks*, 1 La. 309 (1830) (discussing a slave known by jailers because of how frequently he was confined as a runaway and finding such a "vice" of sale.); *Williamson v. Norton*, 7 La.Ann. 393 (1852) (discussing the confinement of a man believed to be a runaway slave who boarded a riverboat, sat at the first table, in the cabin, near the ladies and mingled for seven or eight hundred miles before being taken into custody); *Kennedy v. Mason*, 10

La.Ann. 519 (1855) (discussing the fatal beating of a slave who had run away on numerous prior occasions).

28. *More Trouble Among the Negros*, Daily Picayune, May 17, 1867, *available at* Colored Police - Page 1 | Louisiana Digital Library (last visited May 10,2021) (describing a protest of over one hundred and fifty Black workers).

29. *See* Glorida J. Brown-Marshall, *She Took Justice the Black Woman, Law and Power 1619 to 1969* 59 (2021); *See also William Hayes Inducted Into The Randolph Society*, RandolphSociety.Org, Feb. 7, 2020, *available at* William Hayes inducted into The Randolph Society – The Randolph Society (last visited April 6, 2022).

30. Andrew Dunford, was a Black physician who owned a sugar plantation and over eighty slaves at the peak of his operations at St. Rosalie Plantation in Plaquemines Parish, Louisiana. Henry Washington was a Black plantation owner who owned slaves at the Orange Grove Plantation in Port Allen, Louisiana. *See* "Remembrances Collection," p.11 (March 2000); At one time, Josephine Decuir, a black woman of wealth, owned over one hundred slaves. Feeling her wealth entitled her to privileges, she purchased a first class ticket and sat in the "Ladies" section of the steamship. After being removed and ordered to the section reserved for blacks, she sued. In 1877, the SCOTUS, despite the Civil Rights Act of 1875 that guaranteed equal access in transportation, ruled that common carriers could discriminate based on race. *See Hall v. Decuir*, 95 U.S. 485 (1877); "[S]ome [free men of color]...owned slaves." Mary Gehman, *The Free People of Color of New Orleans* 3 (2014).

31. *The Contemplated Negro Revolt in Lafayette, Parish*, Daily Picayune, Sept. 5, 1840, *available at* Slave revolt is reported and put down in Louisiana in 1840. | Louisiana Digital Library (last visited May 10, 2021).

32. Carolyn Kolb, *A Creole Activist in the Age of Jim Crow The Work of Alice Moore Dunbar-Nelson*,64 Parishes (Winter 2020), *available at* A Creole Activist in the Age of Jim Crow | 64 Parishes (last visited May 3, 2021) (mentioning free people of color as Confederate supporters); "[S]ome [free men of color]...joined the Confederacy in the Civil War." Mary Gehman, *The Free People of Color of New Orleans* 3 (2014); "In Louisiana, the colored creoles... actually fought in the Confederate Army, but were not registered as Negros." W.E. B. Du Bois, *Black Reconstruction in America* 76 (2007).

33. White men were the only people eligible for legislative service at this time. Silence or compliance with the majority view would have been the path of least resistance at the time.

34. The Reconstruction Amendments' Debates, 288 (Alfred Avins ed, 2nd ed. 1974) (40th Cong., 2d. Sess., Jan. 23, 1868).

35. The Reconstruction Amendments' Debates, 113 (Alfred Avins ed, 2nd ed. 1974) (39th Cong., 1st. Sess., Jan. 23, 1866) (Statement of Representative Thaddeus Stevens).

36. The Life and Public Services of Henry Wilson, *available at* https://www.electricscotland.com/history/wilson/chapter18.htm (last visited 09/16/20).

37. The Reconstruction Amendments' Debates, 265 (Alfred Avins ed, 2nd ed.

1974) (39th Cong., 2d Sess., Senate Ex. Doc. No. 2, Jan. 8, 1867)(Statement of John Kasson).

38. *Id.*

39. The Reconstruction Amendments' Debates, 264 (Alfred Avins ed, 2nd ed. 1974) (39th Cong., 2d Sess., Jan. 8, 1867).

40. *Id.*; While Representative Kasson succeeded in securing passage of the resolution in the House, the bill was postponed indefinitely in the Senate.

41. While Black males happen to be the primary mentoring target of 100 BM, the organization does not operate with an exclusion policy. 100 BM serves all youth that apply to their youth enrichment programs. 100 BM offer to those they serve: assistance with the development of leadership skills, mentoring, academic support, health and wellness initiatives and economic empowerment.

42. He is also involved with St. Aloysius Church. Boy Scout Troop 7; Boys and Girls Club of Metro Louisiana, and American Red Cross. Attorney Whitehead wishes "to attract other thought leaders to take this step forward and devote time to improving the lives of others."

43. Mark T. Carleton, *Politics and Punishment The History of the Louisiana State Penal System* 18 (1971).

44. *Id.*

45. Brian M. Davis, *In Search of a Rosenwald School,* 64 Parishes, p. 52 (fall 2021), *available at* In Search of a Rosenwald School - 64 Parishes (last visited April 6, 2022).

46. *See* Gail Thomas, Kenvi Phillips & Stacey Shorter, *A Brief History African-American Historic and Cultural Resource,* 45 (2012), *available at* African-Americans in Prince George's County.pdf (last visited Feb, 21, 2022).

47. Brian M. Davis, *In Search of a Rosenwald School,* 64 Parishes, p. 52 (fall 2021), *available at* In Search of a Rosenwald School - 64 Parishes (last visited April 6, 2022).

48. *Ramos v. La.,* 140 S.Ct. 1390 (2020).

49. *See Connick v. Thompson,* 563 U.S. 51 (2011).

50. *See Flowers v .Mississippi,* 139 S. Ct. 2228 (2019) (Thomas, J., dissenting).

51. LCDC, organized by Henry Schwarzchild and Carl Rachkin, assigned him to work in the firm of Robert Collins, Nils Douglas and Lolis Edward Elie, a firm of three Black lawyers who represented CORE and handled a large volume of civil rights cases from across the state. At the time, CORE was the only national civil rights organization active and with office in Louisiana.

52. This should not be interpreted as a suggestion that Black lawyers did not exist, lacked interest in the cause of civil rights or were incapable of handling civil rights cases during the period of 1950-1970s in Louisiana. These Black lawyers fought valiant and tireless fights during this period. Many of them worked cases with Attorney Sobel. Some, personally or through family, were present at attorney Sobol's 2022 memorial to attest to this. They too are celebrated and recognized as revolutionaries: Robert F. Collins, Nils R. Douglas, Lolis E. Elie, Ernest Jones, John P. Nelson, Etta K. Hearns and Johnnie Jones are some.

53. Attorney Sobol left Louisiana in 1968 shortly after the Duncan decision and returned to Washington to practice law. He also taught at the University of Michigan's law school before returning to Louisiana in 1971. Three years later he founded a civil rights law firm in Washington, D.C. with Michael Trister. In 1991, he returned to Louisiana, where he lived for more than two decades.

54. *See Hicks v. Crown Zellerbach Corporation*, 319 F.Supp. 314, 325 (1970). Attorney Sobol was involved in at least thirty-one employment discrimination cases, either as lead or co-counsel or by filing amicus briefs. *see also Oatis v. Crown Zellerbach Corp.*, 398 F.2d 496 (1968); *U. S. v. Local 189*, 282 F.Supp. 39 (1968);
     Parson v. Kaiser Aluminum & Chemical Corp., 575 F.2d 1374 (1978);
     Williams v. New Orleans S. S. Ass'n, 673 F.2d 74 (1982).

55. *See* Richard Sobol, *Lawyers Constitutional Defense Committee in Louisiana*, in *Voices of Civil Rights Lawyers Reflections From the Deep South, 1964-1980* 218 (Kent Spriggs ed. 2017).

56. *See Local 300 v. McCulloch*, 428 F.2d 396 (5th Cir. 1970).

57. *U.S. v. Goff*, 509 F.2d 825 (1975) (The court found that the underrepresentation was not substantial enough, as defined by the JSSA, to require supplementation of the voter registration list.); *United States v. McDaniels*, 379 F. Supp. 298 (1973) (the court determined that approximately 20% underrepresentation of blacks on voter registration list was not a substantial deviation from a full cross section of the community requirement of the JSSA.).

58. *See Moses v. Washington Parish School Board*, 276 F.Supp. 834 (E.D. La. 1967); *Zanders v. Louisiana State Board of Education*, 281 F.Supp. 747 (1968); *Carter v West Feliciana School Board*, 396 US 226 (1969).

59. *See Wyche v. Post*, 297 F. Supp. 46 (W.D. La. 1969); *Brown v. Post*, 279 F. Supp. 60 (W.D. La. 1968); *U.S. v. Post*, 279 F. Supp. 46 (W.D. La. 1969).

60. *See* Richard Sobol, *Lawyers Constitutional Defense Committee in Louisiana*, in *Voices of Civil Rights Lawyers Reflections From the Deep South, 1964-1980* 218 (Kent Spriggs ed. 2017).

61. *See Hicks v. Weaver*, 302 F. Supp. 619 (E.D. La. 1969); *see also* Richard Sobol, *Lawyers Constitutional Defense Committee in Louisiana*, in *Voices of Civil Rights Lawyers Reflections From the Deep South, 1964-1980* 218 (Kent Spriggs ed. 2017) (Discussing *Hicks v. Weaver*, 302 F. Supp. 619 (E.D. La. 1969).

62. L. W. Davis was the Mayor of Ferriday and, in that capacity, was the sole judge and presiding official of the Mayor's Court of Ferriday. In *Scott v. Davis*, 404 F.2d 1373 (5th Cir. 1968), the defendants complained that their right to a public trial had been denied. They alleged that Mr. Davis: (1) excluded friends and relatives from the courtroom; (2) refused to allow attorneys to see their clients prior to trial and, in at least one instance, an attorney was refused admittance to defend his client until persistent knocking on a locked courtroom door gained admission for him; (3) refused to allow the defendants or their attorneys inspect the municipal ordinances of the city prior to any alleged violation or criminal proceeding, thus depriving them of

their right to notice of potential criminal liability; and, (4) refused to accept bond from professional or personal sureties posted in behalf of petitioners; *see also Whatley v. City of Vidalia*, 399 F.2d 521 (5th Cir. 1968); *Wyche v. La.*, 394 F.2d 927 (5th Cir. 1967); *Wyche v. Hester.*, 431 F.2d 791 (5th Cir. 1970); *State v. Lewis*, 199 So.2d 907 (1967); *State v. Skiffer*, 218 So.2d 313 (1968); Scott v. Davis, 404 F.2d 1373 (5th Cir. 1968); *See Butler v. DC*, 346 F.2d 798 (1965) (where a conviction for not adequately writing a court-ordered essay explaining why police should be respected was revered).

63. Attorney Sobol was arrested for disturbing peace in 1965 on the night Viola Liuzza was murdered as he participated in a protest outside the white house urging President to take action to protect Southern civil rights workers and to enforce civil rights.

64. RRAAM exists to educate visitors about the history and culture of African Americans in the rural communities of south Louisiana through the collection, preservation, and interpretation of art, artifacts, and historic buildings. Further information about RRAAM can be located at: River Road African American Museum

65. *Eubanks v. Louisiana*, 356 U.S. 584, 588 (1958).

66. *Id.*

67. *See* Laura Sullivan, *Favors, Inconsistencies Taint Angola Murder Case*, Nat'l Pub. Radio (Oct. 28, 2008).

68. *See generally* Butler & Henderson, *Dying to Tell: Angola, Crime, Consequence, Conclusion at Louisiana State Penitentiary* (1992).

69. Martin Luther King, Jr., *Why We Can't Wait* 86-87 (1963).

70. James Forman, *Juries and Race in the Nineteenth Century*, 113 Yale L.J. 895, 908-9 (2004) (citations omitted).

71. *See* James Forman, *Juries and Race in the Nineteenth Century*, 113 Yale L.J. 895 (2004) (citations omitted).

72. The Court reviewed a state attempt to regulate the fugitive slave process in *Prigg v. Pennsylvania* and upheld the constitutionality of the Fugitive Slave Act, striking down a Pennsylvania law as interfering with a slaveowner's right of recapture under federal law. After Prigg, the abolitionists' principal approach was to withdraw any state support for slaveowners seeking to enforce the Fugitive Slave Act and capture blacks, making both the kidnapping of free blacks and the recovery of slaves more difficult.

73. Following a challenge by defense attorneys, the indictment was amendment to remove the alias. *See State v. Montgomery*, 181 So.2d 756 (1966).

74. Sixth periodic report submitted by the United States of America under article 19 of the Convention pursuant to the simplified reporting procedure, R. No. CAT/C/USA/6, at 23 (April 5, 2022), *available at* G2230146.pdf (ecoi.net) (last visited May 24, 2022).

75. Southern Center for Human Rights, *A Guide to Helping Loved Ones in Georgia Prisons* (5th ed. 2009), *available at* AdvocacyHandbook1109.pdf (schr.org) (last visited July 18, 2024).

76. Louisiana Informational Handbook for Friends and Families of People in

Prison, *available at* handbook4friends.familiesofinmates_9_11_19.pdf (louisiana.gov) (last visited July 18, 2024).

77. Prison Activist Resource Center, Resources, *available at* Resources | Prison Activist Resource Center (last visited July 18, 2024).

78. Prison Policy Initiative, Advocacy Toolkit, *available at* Advocacy Toolkit | Prison Policy Initiative (last visited July 18, 2024).

79. The Reconstruction Amendments' Debates, 81 (Alfred Avins ed, 2nd ed. 1974) (38th Cong., 2d Sess., June 21, 1864) (Statement of James Ashley).

80. Rape cases involving Black defendants and White victims have a special history in the south. *See* Derrick A. Bell, Jr, *Race, Racism and American Law* 949 (1973). "Historically, the South's system of segregation had been designed primarily to prevent interracial sex. The taboo against sex between black men and white women was central to whites' control of blacks, even as white supremacy authorized unlimited white male access to black women." *See* Shannon Frystak, *Oretha Castle Haley (1939-1987)*, in *Louisiana Women Their Lives and Times* 314 (Janet Allured & Judith F. Gentry eds., 2009); The black woman was a "breeder of slaves." Glorida J. Brown-Marshall, *She Took Justice the Black Woman, Law and Power 1619 to 1969* 37 (2021); "Her womb was industry." Glorida J. Brown-Marshall, *She Took Justice the Black Woman, Law and Power 1619 to 1969* 37 (2021); A study of these cases found, "compared to other rape defendants, blacks convicted of raping white women were disproportionately found guilty and sentenced to death." Derrick A. Bell, Jr, *Race, Racism and American Law* 949 (1973); One study revealed that jurors were less likely to render a guilty verdict in rape trials when the complainant is a black woman." Juan. F. Perea, Richard Delgado, Angela P. Harris, Jean Stefancic & Stephanie M. Wildman, *Race and Races Cases and Resources for a Diverse America* 934 (2015) (Suggesting that the results could be due to stereotypes of black women being over sexual).

81. *The Patton v. U.S.*, 281 U.S. 276, 302 (1930) court said:

If a deficiency of one juror might be waived, there appears to be no good reason why a deficiency of eleven might not be; and it is difficult to say why, upon the same principle, the entire panel might not be dispensed with, and the trial committed to the court alone. It would be a highly dangerous innovation, in reference to criminal cases, upon the ancient and invaluable institution of trial by jury, and the constitution and laws establishing and securing that mode of trial, for the court to allow of any number short of a full panel of twelve jurors, and we think it ought not to be tolerated.

82. *Johnson v. Louisiana*, 406 U.S. 356 (1972).

83. *Apodaca v. Oregon*, 406 U.S. 404 (1972).

84. *Apodaca* was a 4-1-4 decision. Both of the groups of four Justices determined the rule should be the same for federal and state trials. Justice Powell differed. Justice Powell believed there to be a distinction between state and federal standards governing the right to a jury trial. In his view, the Sixth Amendment required a unanimous verdict, while the 14th Amendment did not incorporate that requirement. Justice Powell was the swing vote so his posi-

tion became the law. The opinion held that there was no constitutional right to a unanimous verdict – based on the opinion of only one Justice.

85. *Ramos v. Louisiana*, 140 S.Ct. 1390, 1397 (2020).

86. In an article I wrote years before the SCOTUS put an end to split juries, I observed the poor reasoning in the opinion and must of the same critique appear in the *Ramos* decision. *See* Angela A. Allen-Bell, *How the Narrative About Louisiana's Non-Unanimous Criminal Jury System Became A Person Of Interest In The Case Against Justice In The Deep South*, 67 Mercer L. Rev. 585, 601-606 (2016). This is not to suggest that I inspired the outcome in *Ramos*. It is only to suggest the shortcomings of *Apadaca* were glaring and they should not have been overlooked as long as they were.

87. Besides a dissent by Justice Douglas in *Johnson v. Louisiana*, 406 U.S. 356 (1972), the jury unanimity decisions have failed to give adequate attention to the meaning of the science. Justice Douglas explained that split juries strip the jury minority of its power to persuade the majority to acquit or to exercise caution by convicting the defendant of a lesser included offense. He also expressed that unanimity operates as a check against hasty factfinding. He further concluded that split juries favored the prosecution Although Justice Douglas did not rely on much empirical data, he did refer to studies conducted by noted jury specialists Harry Kalven and Hans Zeisel. He insisted that verdict unanimity operated to ensure substantial participation by all groups in the criminal justice system.

88. *Ramos v. Louisiana*, 140 S.Ct. 1390, 1405 (2020).

89. *See* Glorida J. Brown-Marshall, *She Took Justice the Black Woman, Law and Power 1619 to 1969*, 73 (2021).

90. *See* Glorida J. Brown-Marshall, *She Took Justice the Black Woman, Law and Power 1619 to 1969*, 103 (2021).

91. COINTELPRO started in 1956 to disrupt the activities of the Communist Party of the United States. In the 1960s, it was expanded to include a number of domestic groups that espoused a civil rights agenda. COINTELPRO was a series of covert, and often illegal projects conduct by the United States FBI and aimed at surveilling, infiltrating, discrediting and disrupting American political organizations and other voices of dissent; *See* Anthony Summers, Official and Confidential The Secret Life of J. Edgar Hoover (1993); *See also* Angela A. Allen-Bell, *The Incongruous Intersection of the Black Panther Party and the Ku Klux Klan*, 39 Seattle U. L. Rev. 1157 (2016); Angela A. Allen-Bell, *A Prescription for Healing a National Wound: Two Doses of Executive Direct Action Equals a Portion of Justice and a Serving of Redress for America & The Black Panther Party*, 5 Univ. Miami Race & Soc. Justice L.Rev. 1 (2015); Angela A. Allen-Bell, *Activism Unshackled & Justice Unchained: A Call to Make a Human Right Out of One of the Most Calamitous Human Wrongs to Have Taken Place on American Soil*, 7 J. of Law & Social Deviance 125 (2014).

92. *See* New Orleans During the Civil War (Teacher's Guide), The Historic New Orleans Collection (2016), p. 17, *available at* LessonPlan_CivilWar.pdf (hnoc.org) (last visited 4/27/21) (emphasis added).

93. Pursuant to the revisions to Supreme Court Rule XXIII, Section 23(a)(1), effective May 1, 2020, "once the Commission files a notice of hearing as provided for in Section 4 of this rule and the respondent judge either files an answer or the time for filing an answer has expired, ... the pleadings, orders, and evidence filed into the record of the proceedings shall be public record, subject to the right of the hearing officer or the Commission to issue a protective order in accordance with Section 8(e)." In addition, Supreme Court Rule XXIII, Section 23(a)(5) provides that certain Commission documents are subject to public disclosure "when a judge retires or resigns from judicial office, and thereafter qualifies to run for another elective public office," and Supreme Court Rules XXXIX and XL provide that certain documents in financial disclosure matters before the Commission shall be matters of public record.

94. *See Knapper v. Connick,* 681 So.2d 944, 950-51 (1996).

95. *See Knapper v. Connick,* 681 So.2d 944, 951, n. 16 (1996); In *Imbler v.Pachtman,* 424 U.S. 409 (1976), "the United States Supreme Court suggested that prosecutors guilty of misconduct may be punished criminally for the willful violation of constitutional rights under 18 U.S.C. § 242. In an appropriate case, prosecutorial misconduct might also be punishable pursuant to our state criminal statutes.").

96. The ODC does not have to prove a violation "beyond a reasonable doubt." They have to meet the lower burden of "clear and convincing evidence." The hearing committee chairperson may approve, modify, or disapprove the recommendation of disciplinary counsel, or direct that the matter be investigated further.

97. At the disciplinary hearing stage, the ODC bears the burden of proof.

98. The Board can recommend the imposition of suspension, disbarment or permanent disbarment.

99. In matters in which the Board determines to dismiss formal charges or issue a public reprimand, the Court will review the Board's determination only on appeal. The Court must review a Board recommendation to suspend, disbar or permanently disbar.

100. The Court may, however, require briefs and/or oral argument. In the event objections to the Board's report and recommendation are filed, the matter shall be assigned for oral argument and notice will be sent to the parties.

101. There were three players involved with Thompson's prosecution, but Thompson appears to place greater culpability on James "Jim" Williams. Thompson's suit also named: then D.A. Harry Connick; his successor D.A. Eddie Jordon; ADA Eric Dubelier; ADA Gerry Deegan. He accused them of withholding a crime lab report that contained the blood type of the perpetrator and then using this evidence at his 1985 trial with full knowledge that that blood type did not match Thompson; Relative to his complaint, 34 USCA § 12601 reads, in pertinent part:

    (a) Unlawful conduct

    It shall be unlawful for any governmental authority, or any agent thereof, or any person acting on behalf of a governmental authority, to engage in a pattern or practice of conduct by law enforcement officers or by officials or employees of any governmental agency with responsibility for the administration of juvenile justice or the incarceration of juveniles that deprives persons of rights, privileges, or immunities secured or protected by the Constitution or laws of the United States.

(b) Civil action by Attorney General

Whenever the Attorney General has reasonable cause to believe that a violation of paragraph (1) has occurred, the Attorney General, for or in the name of the United States, may in a civil action obtain appropriate equitable and declaratory relief to eliminate the pattern or practice.

See The U.S. Department of Justice, *Justice Department Announces Investigations of the Handling of Sexual Assault Allegations by the University of Montana, the Missoula, Mont., Police Department and the Missoula County Attorney's Office,* DOJ (May 1, 2012), https://www.justice.gov/opa/pr/justice-department-announces-investigations-handling-sexual-assault-allegations-university (last visited Sept. 23, 2022).

Further support is found in the DOJ's investigation of the Ferguson Police Department following the shooting of Michael Brown. That complaint states under a section asserting violations of § 14141 that "Defendant, its agents, and persons acting on its behalf have intentionally *prosecuted* and resolved municipal violations in the City of Ferguson in a manner that violates due process and equal protection requirements." See United States v. City of Ferguson, Civil Complaint 4:16-cv-00180, (Feb. 10, 2016), https://www.justice.gov/opa/file/823486/download.

102. State disclosure of exculpatory evidence is established by *Brady v. Maryland,* 373 U.S. 83 (1963). In *Brady,* the SCOTUS ruled that withholding evidence favorable to the defendant is a violation of a defendant's constitutional rights under the due process clause of the Fourteenth Amendment. This decision requires prosecutors to share with the defense any evidence that is potentially exculpatory and is material to either the guilt or punishment of the defendant.

103. Civil Rights Division's reporting portal: https://civilrights.justice.gov/.

104. The foundations of this body of law are the Charter of the United Nations and the Universal Declaration of Human Rights, adopted by the General Assembly in 1945 and 1948, respectively.

105. The late George Jackson was both a successful organizer and a respected prison intellectual. In 1970, he released *Soledad Brother,* a book that exposed prison conditions to a captive world audience. While this endeared many people to him, this cemented his adversarial relationship with the prison staff. George Jackson was also an activist, the founder of the BGF, a member of the BPP and, as a result, a target of J. Edgar Hoover's COINTELPRO program.

In the early 1970s, John Clutchette was incarcerated at California Correctional Training Facility at Soledad. He was housed on the tier with George Jackson. At the time, there were documented racial problems inside the facility, as well as allegations of excessive force and other abuses on the part of the guards. In this climate, three Black inmates were murdered by a white guard, Black inmate witnesses were not allowed to testify at trial and the guard was not prosecuted. Shortly thereafter, In January 1970, John Mills, a white prison guard was murdered. George Jackson, John Clutchette and Freeda Drumgo were accused of Officer Mills' murder and, subsequently, indicted in February 1970. The trio became known as the "Soledad Brothers." Clutchette was less than three months away from parole.

Months later, in August 1970, a heavily armed, seventeen-year-old Jonathan Jackson, George's youngest brother, entered the Marion County Courthouse during a trial. Jonathan armed three prisoners before the group left with five hostages, which included the judge and district attorney. In an effort to stop the escape, officers killed Jonathan, the judge and two of the prisoners. A year later, in August 1971, George was killed by San Quentin prison guards, leaving his associates, however distant, to pay for his sins, both real and imagined.

Tensions surrounding the "Soledad Brothers" case were high in the 1970s. When we filed, the case still stirred emotions in some circles. From all appearances, officials deemed the "Soledad Brothers" guilty on the day they were arrested and viewed the surrounding legal process as a mere formality—something akin to a pit stop on the way to their final destination toward literal or figurative death in prison. Efforts were made to ensure the death or permanent incarceration of each of these men. Their attorneys received intimidating visits from the FBI, policy was used to silence these men, and, in instances, the prosecution went beyond the reach of the law to ensure convictions were obtained. Fate would write another ending for Clutchette. In February 1972, Clutchette was acquitted by the all-white jury that presided over his case. He further defied odds when he was granted parole on November 13, 1972. Of note, none of the "Soledad Brothers" were found guilty of the murder of Officer Mills. Also noteworthy is the fact that Clutchette was not charged or convicted in the 1970 Marion County Courthouse matter that was onset by Jonathan Jackson, nor the 1971 Adjustment Center incident that resulted in the death of George Jackson.

Clutchette remained a free man from 1972 until 1980 when he was placed in custody to stand trial for the murder of Robert Bowles. Clutchette was convicted of the Bowles murder in the 1980s and an indeterminate sentence of seven years to life was imposed. Two additional years were added for use of a weapon. The California Penal Code grants parole authority to the California Board of Parole Hearings. A prisoner shall be found unsuitable for and denied parole if it is found that the prisoner will pose an unreasonable risk of danger to society if released from prison. The California Governor had the authority to review parole decisions and reverse or modify them. On November 4, 2016, Governor Brown reversed the Board's parole favorable decision. In so doing, we argued that the governor acted outside the bounds of both state law and human rights tenants. Governor Brown issued written reasons. A number of his observations are sound, such as his recognition that Clutchette: has taken advantage of many self-improvement programs; has generously donated money to charity; has received above average work ratings; has made efforts to improve himself while incarcerated; and, has not been disciplined for serious misconduct since 2008.

We challenged of the governor's opinion, which: (1) involved reliance on the false information in Clutchette's prison records; and, (2) displayed of an animus to, through the parole process, "sentence" or punish Clutchette for the 1970's Soledad murder that he was acquitted of, the 1970 Marion County Incident he was never charged with and the 1971 Adjustment Center Incident he was never charged with. Cluchette had been eligible for parole since 1988. He was granted parole in 2003 and again in 2015 with the involvement of the district attorney on each occasion.

106. It bore the following signatures: Angela A. Allen-Bell, Endorser & Author & Law & Minorities Professor; Danielle Bickham, Author Law & Minorities Student; Chandra Johnson, Author Law & Minorities Student; Brandon-Rashad Kenny, Author Law & Minorities Student; Ryan Thompson, Author Law & Minorities Student.

107. William Fox, *A Soledad Brother: How a Group of Students Hundreds of Miles from California Took on the Cause of an Aging Prisoner*, Voices of Monterey Bay, March 21, 2018.

108. Leonard Peltier, an indigenous activist was arrested in 1976 and later convicted of murdering two FBI agents. The Working Group on Arbitrary Detention received a 2004 complaint involving government misconduct during the trial stage of the case. In 2005, the working group did not reach a finding of arbitrary detention. Years later, an additional complaint was made (asserting a change of circumstances), this time complaining of improprieties with the parole process and alleging improper medical care and abuses relative to his housing assignment. In 2021, the working group requested a response from the United States government. The government replied in February 2022. An arbitrary detention determination was made (under select categories of the International Covenant on Civil and Political Rights).

109. This was a collaborative effort between three advocacy groups: Concerned Citizens of St. John, Inclusive Louisiana and The Descendants Projects.

110. See the Universal Declaration of Human Rights for a list of the thirty rights: Universal Declaration of Human Rights | United Nations.

111. *See* UN Huma Rights Office of the High Commissioner, *Individual Complaint Procedures under the United Nations Human Rights Treaties*, Fact Sheet No. 7/Rev.2 (2013), *available at* 1313354_HR_Fact_Sheet_Rev.2_ENG.pdf (ohchr.org) (last visited April 20, 2022).

112. The special procedures consist of a number of experts who bear different titles such as special rapporteurs, special representatives, independent experts or working groups and whose mandates were received from the Human Rights Council.

113. Klaus Hufner, German Commission for UNESCO, How to File Complaints on Human Rights Violations (2010), available at Hüfner_how_to_file_complaints_on_human_rights_violations.pdf (unesco.de) (last visited April 20, 2022).

114. Open Society Foundations, *Drafting Complaints to the United Nations Human Rights Committee and Committee against Torture* (2018), *available at* litigation-toolkit-torture-20180427.pdf (justiceinitiative.org) (last visited April 20, 2022) (Discussing Individual communications to committees).

115. After the law changed, the book was updated to discuss how the law was changed. The updated edition presents a very incomplete summary of the advocacy efforts and it fails to properly reflect the contributions of the many individuals who were integral players in the campaign and, in so doing, improperly inflated the roles of a few players. For this reason, I distinguish between the original and the updated versions of the book.

116. Dr. Aiello's original book was also cited by the SCOTUS in *Ramos v. La.,* 140 S.Ct. 1390 (2020).

117. *See Plessy v. Ferguson,* 163 U.S. 537, 551 (1896).

118. *See A Revealing Experiment:Brown v. Board and "The Doll Test",* Naacpldf.org, *available at* Brown v. Board: The Significance of the "Doll Test" (naacpldf.org) (last visited April 13, 2022).

119. *See Brown v Board of Education,* 347 U.S. 483, 494 n.11 (1954).

120. *See McCleskey v. Kemp,* 481 U.S. 279 (1987).

121. Some feel *McCleskey* acts as a substantial barrier to the elimination of racial inequalities in the criminal justice system.

122. He also unsuccessfully argued that the Eighth Amendment's ban on cruel and unusual punishment had been violated.

123. *See* Angela A. Allen-Bell, *Perception Profiling & Prolonged Solitary Confinement Viewed Through The Lens of The Angola 3 Case: When Prison Officials Become Judges, Judges Become Visually Challenged and Justice Becomes Legally Blind,* 39 Hastings Const. L.Q. 763 (2012) (Lead Article).

124. Thomas Aiello, *Non-Unanimous Juries,* 64 Parishes Encyclopedia, *available at* Non-Unanimous Juries - 64 Parishes (last visited April 2024).

125. For many years in the history of the legal academy, those who teach legal writing and analysis have existed in a purgatory of sorts. The title suggests they are law professors like all other law professors, but, in actually, many do not experience parity. Historically, legal writing and analysis professors earn less than doctrinal professors, they sometimes don't share equally in the distribution faculty governance power and they are disproportionately women. At the time of my work on ending split juries, much of this was my existence. I am fortunate to have witnesses a slight change in my lifetime and at my institution. In 2020, the faculty decided to grant legal writing professors parity and tenure eligibility.

126. Louisiana's non-unanimous jury system is thoroughly discussed in my books *Under Indictment: Race, Juries & Justice in Louisiana* and *Diversity in the Jury Box and Beyond: A Formula for Transforming Louisiana Injustice System.*

127. *State v. Melvin Cartez Maxie,* No. 13-CR-72522, (11th JDC Oct. 11, 2018).

128. *State v. Lee,* No. 500-034 & 498-666, Criminal District Court, Parish of Orleans, 2/3/17 was offered as an exhibit.

129. Much of my work as a change agent has been "heart work" that I undertake out of a commitment to a better legal system and not because it is assigned or expected as a part of my official duties as a professor.

130. Military appellate courts have consistently held that the 6th amendment only applies to civilian cases and the military is excluded from this constitutional requirement. The Uniform Code of Military Justice (UCMJ), however, requires only a three-fourths jury vote for a conviction, and only requires a unanimous vote with cases involving capital offense charges.

131. Military and civilian court cases operate under different sets of laws, processes, and sentencings. These differences include court proceedings and regulations where military courts do not always align with the standard set by the US Supreme Court. Supreme Court rulings do not always impact military courts as the US Constitution gives Congress the power to make rules for the military, including a military justice system that does not have the same regulations and protections for service members as civilian defendants have.

132. In January 2023, Dial was sentenced dismissal from the Army but no time in prison after his earlier appeal was denied.

133. "Servicemembers have no constitutional right to an 'impartial jury'. It is not essential that all of the jurors hear the same evidence throughout the same trial to convict, and it is not fatal if several jurors drop out midway through the trial. Military defendants enjoy less robust peremptory strike privileges than their civilian counterparts. They are generally tried by a jury of their superiors, not their peers. There is no right that the jury be drawn from a representative cross-section of the community." Captain Nino C. Monea, *"Reforming Military Juries in the Wake of Ramos v. Louisiana"* 66 Naval L. Rev. 67, 68 (2020) (citations omitted).

134. About "42 states have introduced measures inhibiting conversations about race and the history of structural racism, while 17 have imposed restrictions. In New Hampshire, the state set up a webpage allowing parents and students to lodge complaints against teachers they believe have violated a 2021 law that bans certain teachings on race, racism and sexism. An activist group offered a $500 bounty for the first person to successfully catch a public school teacher breaking the state's law. Some right-wing legislators and school boards are also demanding schools and libraries remove content deemed offensive—with many books related to LGBTQ+ or racism topics." Liane Jackson, *Students are Collateral Damage in America's War on Teachers*, ABA Journal, 25 (June-July 2022).

Chapter 2

1. Promotion and Protection of All Human Rights, Civil, Political, Economic, Social and Cultural Rights, Including the Right to Development, Human Rights and Transitional Justice, Rep. No. A/HRC/49/39, p. 2 (Jan. 12, 2022) (citing General Assembly resolution 67/1, para. 21; and S/2004/616, para. 8.), available at G2200465.pdf (un.org) (last visited May 19, 2022).

2. This should not be interpreted as an exhaustive list or a guarantee of any future results.

3. *Ramos v. Louisiana,* 140 S.Ct. 1390 (2020) was written by Neil Gorsuch.

4. To determine if *Ramos* applied retroactively on federal collateral review, the Court had to first determine if *Ramos* announced a new rule of criminal procedure and, if so, whether that rule fell within an exception for watershed rules of criminal procedure that apply retroactively on federal collateral review. Under the existing precedent, a decision announcing a new rule of criminal procedure ordinarily does not apply retroactively on federal collateral review, but a new rule of criminal procedure applies to cases on *direct* review, even if the defendant's trial has already concluded. The Court identified only one possible exception to that principle. The Court stated that a new procedural rule will apply retroactively on federal collateral review only if it constitutes a "watershed" rule of criminal procedure. The Court concluded that *Ramos* announced a new rule. They further found that the requirement for a unanimous jury vote was not sufficiently "watershed" as to require *Ramos* to be made retroactive. See *Edwards v. Vannoy,* 141 S.Ct. 1547 (2021) written by Justice Kavanaugh.

5. During Phase III, in March 2022, Representative Jason Hughes filed HB 271, which seeks to heal the injuries caused by non-unanimous verdicts.

6. The school was founded by St. Katharine Drexel and the Sisters of the Blessed Sacrament in 1915 under the name Xavier University Preparatory School. Drexel Prep gave Black teenagers in the New Orleans metro area an opportunity to receive a quality Catholic education that would prepare them for life's challenges at a time when segregation was still in effect. In 2013, the name changed to St. Katherine Drexel Preparatory High School, but the mission remained the same. The focus of the program is the development of Christian girls through a harmonious blending of their spiritual, moral, intellectual, emotional, and physical strengths. Prep prepares students to live with compassion, dignity, and responsibility in a constantly evolving world. I am also a proud graduate.

7. *State v. Reddick,* 21-01893, 2022 WL 12338521, p. 6-7 (Oct. 21, 2022)(Griffin, J., dissenting).

8. *State v. Reddick,* 21-01893, 2022 WL 12338521, p. 11 (Oct. 21, 2022)(Genovese, J., concurring in part).

9. The First Amendment states:

   Congress shall make no law respecting an establishment of religion, or prohibiting the free exercise thereof; or abridging the freedom of speech, or of the press; or the right of the people peaceably to assemble, and to petition the government for a redress of grievances.

10. *State v. Read,* 6 La.Ann 227, 227-228 (1851).

11. *Lombard v. La.,* 83 S.Ct. 1122, n.2 (1963).

12. *Id.*

13. *See* Shannon Frystak, *Oretha Castle Haley (1939-1987),* in *Louisiana Women Their Lives and Times* 309 (Janet Allured & Judith F. Gentry eds., 2009).

14. *Cox v. Louisiana*, 85 S.Ct. 453, 462 (1965).
15. In July 2016, East Baton Rouge Parish District Attorney Hillar Moore announced that the majority would not be prosecuted; A federal class-action lawsuit suit, filed on behalf of ninety-two protesters of which Black Lives Matter activist DeRay McKesson was the lead plaintiff, alleged that law enforcement used excessive force during the protests, made arrests without cause and violated demonstrators' civil rights. The protesters involved in the suit were arrested on misdemeanor counts of obstructing a highway during the demonstrations. It was settled for $136,000.00 (intended to cover bail fees, attorney's fees and other costs) and an agreement to expunge records of the arrest. Another group of protesters did not settle their cases. They are scheduled for trial in January 2023.
16. *See* Hilary Coulby, *Advocacy Communications A Handbook for ANEW Members*, 47 (2010), *available at* Microsoft Word - Advocacy Communications - a Handbook for ANEW Members .doc (freshwateraction.net) (last visited April 18, 2022).
17. *Id.*
18. Human rights are rights inherent to all human beings, regardless of race, sex, nationality, ethnicity, language, religion, or any other status. We have human rights simply because we are born. No government, group or individual person has the right to do anything that violates another's rights. Article 27 of the 1948 Universal Declaration of Human Rights states:

    Everyone has the right freely to participate in the cultural life of the community, to enjoy the arts and to share in scientific advancement and its benefits.

    (2) Everyone has the right to the protection of the moral and material interests resulting from any scientific, literary or artistic production of which he is the author.
19. *Nonunanimous* can be viewed at: 02 - Docs - Ben Donnellon (cargo.site) .
20. The video can be located at: Black Jurors: Missing in Action or Missing by Practice? - YouTube .
21. The video can be located at: Black Jurors: Missing in Action or Missing by Practice Symposium - YouTube
22. *Herman's House*, Discussion Guide, POV.org, *available at* Discussion Guide | Herman's House | POV | PBS (last visited April 19, 2022).
23. *Id.*
24. *Id.*
25. *5th Ward Weebie Let Me Find Out (VOTE!) Remix*, Youtube.com, *available at* (412) 5th Ward Weebie Let Me Find Out (VOTE!) Remix - YouTube (last visited April 19, 2022); Tragically, in 2020, 5th Ward Webbie had a heart attack which turned into emergency heart surgery and ultimately heart failure.
26. The artist Emory Douglass used *"All Power to the People"* as the solidarity symbolism synonymous with the raised fist. The raised fist and the words "All Power to The People" impacts most people on an emotional level, making it a very powerful piece of artwork.

27. *L'Union*, founded in 1862. Dr. Louis Charles Roudanez was *L'Union's* primary financier and Paul Trévigne its editor. The paper suspended publication on July 19, 1864.

28. The New Orleans Tribune, organized in 1864, was the successor to L'Union. Louis Charles Roudanez and Paul Trévigne remained at the helm. The Tribune printed the first page in the French of many free blacks and the reverse in the English mainly read and spoken by freedpersons. In 1867 the federal government designated the Tribune an official paper of the United States, one of only two in the state given the responsibility of publishing the authentic texts of laws, administrative announcements, and judicial decisions. The paper was published weekly by 1869 and folded the following year.

29. *See* Hilary Coulby, *Advocacy Communications A Handbook for ANEW Members*, 6 (2010), *available at* Microsoft Word - Advocacy Communications - a Handbook for ANEW Members .doc (freshwateraction.net) (last visited April 18, 2022).

30. *Id.*

31. *Id.*

32. *See* Trent Angers, *The Forgotten Hero of My Lai* 21 (1999).

33. *Id.*

34. In 2004, Judge Edwain Lombard suggested the same in a concurrence:

    The state constitution mandates that judges not engage in conduct that brings the judicial office in disrepute. Those who would write off Judge Ellender's lapse in judgment as a harmless prank requiring only a token sanction do not understand how deeply such an act resonates throughout the African-American community as a harsh reminder of a not too distant past. I believe, however, that educating a sitting judge as to the reality of racial injustice and insensitivity in our daily lives will have more far-reaching consequences than simply removing him. Requiring Judge Ellender to undergo racial sensitivity training sends the message not only to Judge Ellender but to the rest of the country that racial slurs and stereotyping, whether intentional or merely thoughtless, will no longer be tolerated in Louisiana. Incorporation of such training for all judges in Louisiana-white or black-into our continuing legal education could be beneficial in preventing similar infractions of the judicial code of conduct and promoting the impartial administration of justice to all our citizens. Accordingly, I support the sanction crafted by the majority.

    See In re Judge Timothy C. Ellender, 889 So.2d 225 (2004).

35. These are the videos that are shown in the exhibit:

    Reconstruction and Jim Crow Era Life After Emancipation: https://vimeo.com/380655989/3a20dc361c

    Legally Free: https://vimeo.com/380655673/b14b887bdb

    The Hope of Education: https://vimeo.com/380656326/1694d69eb1

    Civil Rights Era

    Let Freedom Ring: https://vimeo.com/380656712/4195e29671

    The Motivation of Law: https://vimeo.com/380673362/effa24a450

    The Key to a Brighter Future: https://vimeo.com/380748078/5a78f2a73

36. The 2001 Report by the Oklahoma Commission to Study the Tulsa Race Riot of 1921 states, "in our interim report in February, 2000 the majority of Commissioners declared that reparations to the historic Greenwood community in real and tangible form would be good public pol icy and do much to re pair the emotional and physical scars of this terrible incident in our shared past."

37. Carol Anderson, *One Person, No Vote* 138 (2019).

38. Ibram X. Kendi, *How to be an Antiracist* (Dec. 2, 2020).

39. Section B of that rule requires that any "person who files a prepared statement which contains data or statistical information shall include in such prepared statement sufficient information to identify the source of the data or statistical information."

40. S. Christie Smith, of the Louisiana Association of Criminal Defense Lawyers, spoke in support of the proposal.

    Pete Adams, executive director of the Louisiana Association of District Attorneys, opposed advancing the bill.

41. *See* La. H.R. 14:32 (2).

42. *Id.*

43. J.P. Morrell, *Reform Without Fear with J.P. Morrell*, Louisiana Lefty Podcast, May 11, 2021, *available at*, 1.13: Reform Without Fear with J.P. Morrell - Louisiana Lefty last visited (Oct. 6, 2022).

44. Prior to settling upon this resolution, Rep. Randal Gaines brought a 2021 bill that aimed to give new trials or a parole option for the over 1,500 people who are still in prison after being convicted by split jury verdicts. It did not make it out the House Judiciary Committee due to opposition from the Louisiana District Attorneys Association. Further legislative efforts are included in Chapter four's "Reparations" discussion.

Post-Script

1. *State v. Snyder*, 750 So.2d 832, 864 (1999) (Lemmon, J., concurring).

2. At its 2022 Midyear Meeting, the ABA House of Delegates approved a new law school accreditation standard. In order to eliminate bias and enhance diversity, the ABA's amended Standard 303(c) requires that "a law school shall provide education on bias, cross-cultural competency, and racism: (1) at the start of the program of legal education, and (2) at least once again before graduation." To fulfill this requirement, law schools must demonstrate that all law students are required to participate in a substantial activity designed to reinforce the skill of cultural competency and their obligation as future lawyers to work to eliminate racism in the legal profession. Presently, bias and cultural literacy training for Louisiana not required for judges elected prior to 2022. Mandatory annual training for all judges is necessary.

3. Niles Haymer, *In Louisiana, Confederate Monuments Have No Place in Front of a Courthouse. Remove All of Them Now*, Bayou Brief, Aug. 21, 2017.

4. Esther Armah is the award-winning journalist, playwright, media communications lecturer and writer who coined the term "Emotional Justice."
5. *See* theaiej.com for further discussion of the emotional language that must be unlearned during this process.
6. Yolo Akili, *The Immediate Need for Emotional Justice*, CrunkFeministCollective.com, Nov. 16, 2011, *available at* The Immediate Need For Emotional Justice (crunkfeministcollective.com) (last visited June 30, 2022).
7. *See* Yolo Akili, *The Immediate Need for Emotional Justice*, CrunkFeminist-Collective.com, Nov. 16, 2011, *available at* The Immediate Need For Emotional Justice (crunkfeministcollective.com) (last visited June 30, 2022).
8. *Id.*
9. *Id.*
10. After various amendments, Louisiana's November 2022 ballot initiative read: "Do you support an amendment to prohibit the use of involuntary servitude except as it applies to the otherwise lawful administration of criminal justice?" Voters rejected this proposal (as did the bill's author in the end).
11. Many other states publicize judicial complaints when the judge is charged, when the judge responds or when the hearing begins.
12. *See State v Perez*, 464 So.2d 737 (1985) (District attorney and district judge were charged with malfeasance and conspiracy to commit malfeasance).